Sanctity and Scandal

The Medieval Religious Houses of Nottinghamshire

The Archdeaconry Research Unit
of the
University of Nottingham

Edited by David Marcombe and John Hamilton

Published in 1998 by

The Continuing Education Press
University of Nottingham, Education Building
University Park, Nottingham, NG7 2RD

ISBN 1 85041 0887

Designed by *Trevor Clayton*

Printed in Great Britain by
Technical Print Services Ltd
Brentcliffe Avenue, Carlton Road, Nottingham, NG3 7AG

Contents

Illustrations

Maps

Tables

Picture Credits

We would like to thank the following for taking photographs, for giving permission for photographs to be taken, for maps, plans and drawings, and for allowing illustrations to be reproduced:

Sheila Chambers, 74; **Trevor Clayton**, front cover (with thanks to the Vicar, Churchwardens and PCC of Holy Trinity church, Lenton), prologue, 4, 16, 17, 18 (with thanks to the Vicar and Churchwardens of the Priory church of Our Lady and St Cuthbert), 32, 33, 37, 68 (with permission of the Provost and Cathedral Council of Southwell Minster), 78, 89, 91; **Les Green**, 53, 62; **Colin Jones,** illustrations at the top of pages 17, 23, 32, 52, 65; **Janet Jones**, illustrations at the top of pages 1, 6, 10, 49, 77, 103, 24, 40; **Local Studies Library, Nottingham**, 20, 28, 67, 84, 86, back cover (with thanks to New York Public Library); **William Nicholson**, 70, 72; **Nottinghamshire Archives Office,** 31(with permission of the Duke of Rutland) (detail photographed by Ian Brown); **Nottinghamshire County Council Tourism and Country Parks,** 45, 46; **Public Records Office,** 7; **private collection**, 34, 57; **Hunter Reid**, illustration on page 11, 12, 19, 64; **Jean Reid**, 10, 11, 63; **Barbara Roper**, 81; **Brian Roweth**, 25; **Anne Tarver,** x, 38 (with thanks to Trevor Foulds); **Sue Terry,** 51

Acknowledgements

P reparing this page was a pleasant exercise as it brought back many happy memories. More important, it reminded us of all those who have assisted in the preparation of *Sanctity and Scandal*. The Archdeaconry Research Unit would like to thank the following people for allowing access to their property or offering information, help and encouragement:

Margaret Bagley, Bernard Beilby, Graham Beaumont, Michael Bishop, Keith Challis, Mr and Mrs Roger Chatterton, Maria Chaworth Musters and the late Major Chaworth Musters, Father Hilary Costello, Dr John Forrester, Elizabeth Hirst, Heidi Jackson, Lieutenant Colonel A. Morton, Enid Oakes, Brenda Penney, Dennis Pearson, Brian Roweth, Father Kevin Smith, Monica Stokes and the staff of the Nottinghamshire Archives Office, the Local Studies Library and the Manuscripts Department of the University of Nottingham. There were many others who opened doors, in more senses than one, and although they have not been mentioned by name it does not lessen the fact of how much we appreciated their involvement.

Producing a book is a complex task and we are very grateful to Margie D'Arcy, Susan Andrews and Rita Poxon for typing the manuscript. The money to pay for the typing was raised by Joy Bristow and Jean Nicholson as a result of their work with the Retford Genealogical Index. We would also like to thank Professor Bernard Hamilton and Dr Sarah Speight for their constructive comments on the content, Dr Anne Tarver for maps, Hunter Reid and Colin Jones for their delightful drawings, Trevor Clayton for design and technical expertise, the Continuing Education Press and our partners and families for their support. Susan Clayton inherited a text which we thought was complete but in fact there still remained a great deal to be done in terms of perfecting the detail. Her skills as a copy editor are greatly appreciated and have contributed in no small degree to making the book what it is. Nevertheless, any remaining errors of fact and interpretation are our own.

All members of the Unit have contributed but some deserve a special mention: Terry Fry for his help and advice in the earlier stages of production, Janet Jones and Sheila Chambers for their hard work as picture editors and John Hamilton for his attention to the text. Finally, we would like to thank David Marcombe who originally suggested the subject and persuaded us to attempt a book; he has guided and encouraged our endeavours through eight very enjoyable years.

Archdeaconry Research Unit
November, 1998

Prologue

Today, when a monk takes up a book on monastic life as it was lived in the past, he tends to read it in the light of personal experience. The men and women who dwelt in these monasteries and religious houses of Nottinghamshire lived their lives in much the same way as monks and nuns do today, though they were much more prominent in society then than we are now. In the past fifty years there have been startling changes in monastic life. In those days, all the services were in Latin just as the monks of old would have known them; nowadays English has replaced Latin. I have shared the daily routine of prayer, chant, readings from scripture with men who were saintly and tried every day to make their ideals shine humbly out of their every action, but of course I have also lived with men who could not maintain such single-minded dedication. Likewise, in each of these religious houses there were men and women unaware of their own holiness, but yet by their example they brightened the world around them with their constant and persistent prayer right up to the moment of death.

In Nottinghamshire there is usually very little left of the buildings or in the records to bear witness to their lives. This book is therefore an exploration. Those who have contributed to it have searched the records and have taken pains to investigate the places where the monasteries stood. Sometimes, as in the case of Welbeck, there are lists of names. These lists can bring home to us in a personal way the fact that the inmates of every house - monks or canons or nuns - were real people. But in most cases we have to content ourselves with the architecture and the economy of the place, and hazard a guess at the people who lived there and what they did. Occasionally, when some scandal occurred, the historical records bring the place alive in a rather unsavoury way. This is to be expected. We are dealing with a period of some four hundred years. Yet we should remember with gratitude that, during the whole of this period, the psalms were being prayed every day, that the old Latin chant, so admired even today and sometimes reaching the top of the hit parade, was the constant source of inspiration in their lives.

In this book, one characteristic that stands out is the hospitality that was shown to travellers. No doubt the monks considered this a duty and a privilege; but it must have been a considerable burden on their finances. The poor and the destitute were often knocking at the door in search of food. I am sure that the monks were pleased to welcome them, as we are today. But the rich and the royal were also to be catered for, and their demands would have stretched resources to the limit and beyond. When the Dissolution came the whole world of monastic life was swept away and the complete secularisation of the sacred took its place. This too, sadly but inevitably, is an important theme in the history of monasticism in this country and indeed of this book. Happily during the past century monasteries have revived throughout the British Isles and are once again flourishing.

Hilary Costello
Monk of Mount Saint Bernard Abbey

November 1998

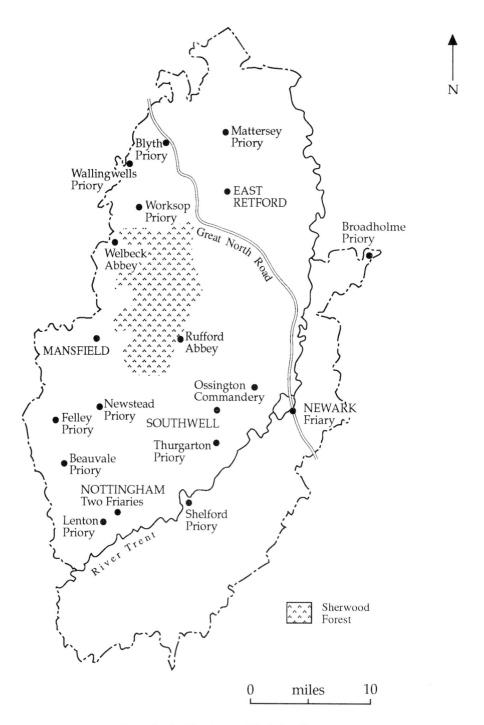

N

Mattersey
Priory

Blyth
Priory

Wallingwells
Priory

EAST
RETFORD

Worksop
Priory

Broadholme
Priory

Great North Road

Welbeck
Abbey

Rufford
Abbey

MANSFIELD

Ossington
Commandery

NEWARK
Friary

Newstead
Priory

Felley
Priory

SOUTHWELL

Thurgarton
Priory

Beauvale
Priory

NOTTINGHAM
Two Friaries

Shelford
Priory

Lenton
Priory

River Trent

Sherwood
Forest

0   miles   10

The medieval religious houses of Nottinghamshire

Setting the Scene

David Marcombe

hristian monasticism had its origins with the 'Desert Fathers' who flourished in the Middle East during the declining years of the Roman Empire. Their life, characterised by asceticism and solitude, was not acceptable to all Christian leaders who soon sought to impose restrictions on the way in which the early hermit monks lived. St Pachomius was one of the first of these monastic reformers, but of greater influence were the Rules attributed to St Augustine of Hippo and St Benedict of Monte Cassino. Augustine's Rule stressed the notions of love and community; Benedict, in a more comprehensive set of regulations, strove to accommodate almost any eventuality which was likely to grow up in the context of communal life. Both were agreed that the monastery, dedicated to the service of God, should offer a positive alternative to the ways of the world, the monastic day being divided up between periods of prayer, work and study. St Benedict's Rule, in particular, was taken up and actively promoted by St Gregory the Great, one of the most energetic and influential of the early Popes. Augustine's Rule became important in the eleventh century, when it was adopted by the Austin Canons, and together with the Rule of Benedict came to dominate the religious life of the Middle Ages; indeed, medieval monks occasionally looked even further back to the example of the Desert Fathers, since Cassian's *Conferences*, required reading in most monasteries, told graphically of their austerities and fierce devotion to God.

Benedict brought the monastic life into Europe, but he did so at a time of great political upheaval when the old Roman Empire was in the process of collapse. Huns, Visigoths and Franks squabbled over the remnants of the Roman world and despite the efforts of Charlemagne to create a new 'Holy' Roman Empire, Christian monks were not always safe from the ravages of pagan barbarians or, indeed, the greed of their own patrons and 'protectors'. In the ninth century, as Charlemagne's bold vision disintegrated, monasticism was under threat as never before. Salvation came from Burgundy, and in particular from the monastery of Cluny founded by William the Pious, Duke of Aquitaine, in 910. Cluny confronted the difficulties of the time in a new and revolutionary fashion. It established a confederacy of Benedictine monasteries with Cluny taking the lead as the 'mother' house; moreover, because of privileges granted by the Papacy, Cluny was able to organise and administer her 'daughters' in a more rigorous fashion than ever before. Under the leadership of a series of remarkable abbots, such as St Odilo and St Hugh the Great, the first religious order had been born. But there were difficulties. The Cluniac solution, bold and successful though it was, represented a decided shift from the ideology of St Benedict who had envisaged the autonomy of individual houses as a prime concern; moreover, Cluny soon established a reputation for worldliness and wealth which conflicted with the simple spiritual life advocated by the founding fathers. By the end of the eleventh century, in a more stable political environment, there were those who were anxious to rediscover first principles.

The twelfth century was an age of spiritual ferment throughout Europe, the reaction against Cluny being a manifestation of this rather than a cause. In England the Norman Conquest of 1066 was a major catalyst for change. England already had its fair share of Saxon monasteries, many of them in origin Celtic foundations, though there were none of these in Nottinghamshire. The Normans had little sympathy for this uneasy and peculiarly English compromise with the past. Between 1066 and 1100 many new monasteries were founded, mostly small dependencies of Benedictine houses in Normandy, the so-called 'alien' priories of which Nottinghamshire had one example at Blyth. Then, between 1100 and 1160, the trickle of new foundations turned into a flood as new religious orders, most of which had their origins on the Continent, made their impact. Amongst the early comers the Augustinian and Premonstratensian canons were not monks in the true sense of the word because, while they lived according to a rule, they were expected to work in the world serving parochial cures. They were encouraged by bishops who were trying

1

to evangelise areas where there was a shortage of clergy, a problem particularly acute in northern England. Augustinian houses were often small and sometimes simply adjuncts to existing parish churches, so they were also popular with secular patrons who wished to establish a monastic community at modest cost. The Augustinians, who were the first of the new orders to make an appearance in England, were sometimes called the black canons; and the Premonstratensians, who saw themselves as a reformed branch of the order, were known as the white canons. By mid-century the orders of canons regular had established houses in Nottinghamshire at Worksop, Felley, Thurgarton, Newstead, Shelford and Welbeck. They were by far the most profound monastic influence on the county.

The habit of a canon regular of St Augustine

Monks of a more traditional sort came into Nottinghamshire when the black-habited Cluniacs colonised Lenton in the early twelfth century. Of the new orders, representing a return to pristine Benedictine values, the Cistercians, or white monks, were undoubtedly the most prolific. Stemming from Citeaux in France and inspired by their great leader St Bernard of Clairvaux, the Cistercians had learned much from the Cluniacs in terms of organisational matters but they did not, initially, embrace their wealth and love of luxury. The Cistercian code was marked by austerity of life and architecture and because of this perceived purity, young men were moved to join them and patrons were inspired to create endowments. They were indeed the greatest success story of a remarkable age and Nottinghamshire was to become home to one Cistercian house at Rufford. Similar to the Cistercians in terms of their austerity, but unique in terms of their monastic architecture,

were the Carthusians, the followers of St Bruno, who had established a monastery at La Grande Chartreuse, near Grenoble. Like the Cistercians they wore white as a symbol of their purity of life but they rejected communal living in favour of assemblages of individual hermitages, a layout best seen today in England at Mount Grace Priory, Yorkshire. Their solitary Nottinghamshire house, at Beauvale, was a late foundation established in 1343.

The habit of a Cluniac monk

The last of the religious orders to make an appearance in the twelfth century was in some ways the most interesting and certainly the only one to be English in its origins; the Gilbertines, who drew their inspiration from a Lincolnshire man, St Gilbert of Sempringham. Gilbert was interested in developing a religious life for women, but he understood they would always require the services of male priests to allow them to partake of the sacraments. Therefore he reverted to an idea which had been popular amongst the Celtic Christians, that of a 'double house' incorporating both men and women, suitably segregated for the sake of decency. Gilbert incurred some opposition, notably from St Bernard who was gravely suspicious of the involvement of women, but he persisted and established a series of monasteries which were most prolific in his native Lincolnshire. Nottinghamshire had one representative of the order at Mattersey, though it is doubtful if this was ever a double house in the true sense of the word. Gilbert was unusual in his concern for women religious because out of the thirteen monasteries of Nottinghamshire only two, Broadholm and Wallingwells, were directed specifically to nuns and they were amongst the poorest in the county. Also founded in the twelfth century were a number of hospitals, which were often run according to a quasi-monastic regime, and a commandery of the Knights of St John of Jerusalem, a local manifestation of the great crusading ideal which was such an important spiritual force during the period.

The Nottinghamshire monasteries, which represent a remarkable variety, were founded by the great Anglo-Norman feudal lords of the twelfth century, the Peverils, the de Gaunts, the Deyncourts and de Lovetots. Looked at on a map it is remarkable to see how many of them were grouped to the west of the Trent, in the bounds of Sherwood Forest, suggesting that these patrons were not giving of their best agricultural land in their foundation charters. But why did they do it? As already stated, the age was one of high spiritual awareness characterised by the crusades and the reform of the Papacy; and on a local level charismatic personalities such as St Ailred of Rievaulx and St Hugh of Lincoln must have brought the message of Christ before a wide spectrum of the English nobility and gentry, if not their poorer neighbours too. But there were also practical considerations. The prosperity of the Norman baronage, evident in castle building as well as the foundation of monasteries, enabled them to engage in competition with their rivals and to possess one's own priory brought considerable social prestige. It was a place where ancestors could lie entombed in splendour and where a perpetual round of liturgy could be carried out for the benefit of the souls of the living and the dead. In short, it bestowed the accolade of social respectability in this world and the ultimate insurance policy in the next.

The years up to 1300 were a period of stability and expansion for the new monastic foundations of Nottinghamshire. Endowments increased as people less exalted than the original founders strove to make their mark as patrons. Building work went on apace; and we must assume that the aesthetic contribution of the monasteries in terms of the output of *scriptoria* and the development of Gregorian chant also flourished, though firm evidence for this sort of activity is sadly lacking. What was new in the thirteenth century, and again strengthened the religious movement as a whole, was the advent of the friars who brought a new ideology to enliven the monastic world. With the exception of the canons regular and the military

orders, who had distinct roles to fulfil outside the cloister, monks were generally speaking introspective, or at least they made their contribution to the welfare of society by means of prayer rather than direct action. At the end of the twelfth century two remarkable individuals, St Francis and St Dominic, reacted against this, suggesting that religious persons should be active in the world in a whole variety of ways. Francis emphasised care of the poor and sick; Dominic preaching and education. In the first half of the thirteenth century the Franciscan and Dominican friars swept across Europe in the same way as their Cistercian counterparts had done a hundred years earlier; and as there had been many orders of monks, so there were many varieties of friars - Carmelites, Trinitarians and Friars of the Sack. Nottinghamshire was less well endowed with friaries than many other counties, largely because of the absence of sizeable towns to which friars tended to gravitate. Nottingham established Franciscan and Carmelite friaries in the thirteenth century; and Newark obtained a house of Franciscan Observants soon before the Dissolution.

The friaries represented the end of the great age of monastic expansion. By 1400 the situation had changed dramatically. The King, growing suspicious of landed endowments passing into the hands of the church, passed the Statute of Mortmain in 1279 which effectively slowed up donations to religious institutions by requiring a license for each new land grant. The war with France, which broke out in 1337 and turned into a long and bitter affair, caused suspicion to be directed against monastic houses which were seen to have a close French affiliation, particularly the alien priories and the Cluniac order. The Black Death of 1349 saw the population of England collapse by a half or a third and brought widespread economic upheaval in its wake. Monasteries which had concentrated on demesne farming in the early years of their existence, providing food to supply an ever increasing population, had to readjust to the role of rentiers in the late Middle Ages, leasing their lands for the best price they could get. And finally, and perhaps most significant over the long term, attitudes began to change. At Oxford the heretical theologian John Wycliffe started to express notions about church reform which left little room for some of the ideas traditionally expressed by the monks; moreover, he looked at the extensive estates held by the monasteries and concluded that it was within the power of

3

the King to expropriate them if he could find a better use for the property, a notion not difficult to justify during the troubled years of the French wars. Partly because of Wycliffe's ideas, spread by his followers the Lollards, attitudes in society experienced a decisive change, amply illustrated by Chaucer's critical portrayal of monks and friars in *The Canterbury Tales*. People became preoccupied with a much more personal faith and a more personal attitude to salvation. Communities of monks interceding for the welfare of society at large were seen to have less relevance than the relationship of the individual with God.

Despite these changes, the day-to-day life of the medieval monk had altered little since the days of St Benedict. The environment of the monastery owed much to the design of a Roman villa with its church and all of its principal buildings arranged around a central cloister; virtually all of the orders adhered to this basic plan with only the Carthusians breaking step to accommodate their hermit-like cells. The main *raison d'etre* of a monk was still the *opus dei,* the eight daily services spanning Matins to Compline which provided the focus and rhythm of his life. Beyond that he could contribute to the well-being of his house in various specific ways, perhaps working with books, guests, scholars, the poor or the management of estates. For a man with administrative ambitions there was a ladder of promotion to climb, through the offices of sacrist or cellarer, which culminated in election as prior or abbot of his house; and then he would move into the ranks of the gentry, receiving royal commissions from time to time and perhaps entertaining the King or great nobles when they visited his abbey. Administrative responsibilities, indeed, must often have diverted the attention of senior monks from the task which they had set themselves in life. It is particularly ironic to imagine a succession of thirteenth century priors attempting to control the unruly tournament at Blyth, armed only with the blunt instrument of excommunication.

People in the Middle Ages, and today, have been fascinated by the quality of life lived within the cloister, specifically the extent to which the great monastic ideals of poverty, chastity and obedience were carried out in practice. All monasteries were subject to Visitation or disciplinary censure of some sort, either from their own internal superiors as in the case of the Cistercians, Cluniacs and

Premonstratensians, or from diocesan bishops as with the Benedictines and Augustinians. In Nottinghamshire this latter role was carried out by the archbishops of York, since the county represented the southernmost portion of their far-flung diocese. The problem for the historian is that all of these visitational sources were specifically directed to the discovery of abuses; what had gone wrong as opposed to what was going right. Thus, from the earliest times onwards we are confronted in the records with a minority of monks and nuns who committed sexual misdemeanours; who were quarrelsome or dishonest; or who in some other way circumvented the rigours of their rule, even down to sporting inappropriate tonsures or falling asleep during services. There were houses which endured real

A brooding figure from the choir stalls at Thurgarton

disciplinary crises from time to time (Newstead, Welbeck and Thurgarton all experienced at least one), but on close examination this is often found to be the result of poor leadership provided by an abbot or prior who, for some reason or another, had temporarily lost control. Beyond that there were also underlying changes in attitude which, over a period of time, moved the monks away from the ideals of their founders. The Cistercian order provides a good example of this. Established in the twelfth century under extremely rigorous directives, by the later Middle Ages the order had waxed rich as sheep farmers and many of its monasteries were pursuing a much more relaxed lifestyle with special 'meat kitchens' built to circumvent the almost entirely vegetarian diet of the pioneer years. If these occasional scandals and changes in attitude caused people to be cynical about life in the cloister, they would have done well to have borne in mind individuals such as Walter Hilton, the great fourteenth century mystic, associated with Thurgarton Priory or the Reformation martyr St Robert Lawrence, associated with Beauvale. Certainly sanctity and scandal are to be found in measure, but it could be that the typical medieval monk neither climbed the heights nor plumbed the depths. He probably saw his life as a career in the service of God and a relatively secure and comfortable one in the context of the rough and ready society which existed around him.

Many of these issues, particularly the growing suspicion of the monastic orders and the vulnerability of their endowments, were to be brought into sharp focus by the events of the early sixteenth century. By then there was already a long history of the suppression of small, corrupt or alien religious houses whose endowments it was believed could be better employed elsewhere. Cardinal Wolsey was especially active in this direction in the 1520s, diverting monastic resources to his new University foundation Cardinal College, Oxford. Thus, when Henry VIII parted company with the Roman Catholic church over the issue of his divorce from Catherine of Aragon, it was not long before the monasteries came onto the agenda of the reformers, actively encouraged by the Protestant Thomas Cromwell. In 1535 a comprehensive survey of church wealth, including the monasteries, was drawn up in the *Valor Ecclesiasticus*. This was followed by a survey of the state of morality in the monasteries, a fragment of which (fortunately including Nottinghamshire) has survived in the form of the *Compendium Compertorum*. It must be said that this latter source gives a uniquely unfavourable report on the county, with many monks deemed guilty of crimes such as fornication and sodomy; the extent to which it is accurate is still a matter of legitimate debate, but certainly it is clear that Cromwell's Visitors were out to do the monks no favours. In 1536 an Act was passed suppressing all monasteries with a net income of less than £200 *per annum* (which accounted for the majority of Nottinghamshire houses), though some were allowed to continue because of various exemptions. At this point the Lincolnshire Rising

and the Pilgrimage of Grace erupted to stop the reformers, briefly, in their tracks, but following the defeat of the rebels the process of dissolution continued with fresh pace, now directed to the larger houses, beyond the scope of the 1536 Act. By 1540, due to a policy of enforced surrenders pursued by Cromwell's agents, English monasticism was no more. In this unhappy saga two Nottinghamshire houses suffered more than most - Beauvale, where Prior Robert Lawrence was executed for treason in 1535; and Lenton, where Prior Nicholas Heath suffered a similar fate in 1538. Lawrence was beatified by the Catholic Church in 1886 and canonised in 1970 as one of the Forty Martyrs of England and Wales. He is the only saint to be directly associated with the religious houses of the county.

The aftermath of the Dissolution brought rewards to the gentry, many of whom had established themselves as tenants of monastic estates in the years following the Black Death. Some monasteries - notably Newstead, Welbeck and Rufford - reinstated themselves as country houses; others were left to the mercy of the elements to decay and deteriorate over a period of time. For the monks the picture was equally variable. Some managed to obtain further religious preferment; others eked out a precarious existence on the pensions granted to them by the Court of Augmentations. What was certain was that things would never be quite the same again. The heritage of five hundred years had been obliterated in less than a decade.

Today physical reminders of the monastic presence in Nottinghamshire are sadly few and far between, but they are enough to conjure a picture of what it must have been like. Worksop Priory, for example, still retains its magnificent Norman nave, a stately gatehouse from the fourteenth century and, for those who wish to travel across the Atlantic to New York, a fine illuminated psalter produced in the monastic *scriptorium*. The pages that follow provide a catalogue of what the religious houses of Nottinghamshire can offer to the historian; to the lover of art and architecture; and to the pilgrim. Though the county may lack the splendours of a Rievaulx or a Fountains, it is by no means devoid of accessible monastic remains where one can still feel the power of the spirit which inspired the first monks and sustained their successors through the years of sanctity and scandal.

Economy and Finance

John Hamilton

This chapter compares the varying experiences of the thirteen monasteries of Nottinghamshire and seeks to elicit common strands in their economic and financial histories. Much of our information comes from two comprehensive surveys of ecclesiastical property: the *Taxatio* of Pope Nicholas IV dated 1291 and the *Valor Ecclesiasticus* of King Henry VIII produced some 250 years later just before the Dissolution and indeed as an aid to it. As evidence, both suffer from the fact that they were drawn up for taxation purposes. Then as now, tax avoidance was practised. Moreover, not all types of income or wealth were taxable. Perhaps more importantly, the *Taxatio* makes no mention of deductions from income, which according to the *Valor* could reach as much as a third of gross income, as at impoverished Wallingwells.

The broad picture painted by the two valuations is of a huge variation in wealth between the monasteries: see Table 1. Lenton had 30 times the income of Felley in 1291, when the three largest houses - Lenton, Thurgarton and Worksop - accounted for well over half Nottinghamshire's total monastic income. The three poorest (Felley and the two nunneries, Broadholm and Wallingwells) got just 3.5 per cent of it. In terms of wealth, therefore, no monastery was typical.

Despite its wealth, Lenton was not among the richest monasteries in England; Glastonbury and Westminster Abbeys both had ten times its income. The nunneries' poverty, on the other hand, was typical of nunneries everywhere. As a whole the county's monasteries were of modest wealth, representing the general economic position of Nottinghamshire in the kingdom. To an extent this was due to their being mostly sited on the poorer forest soils to the north and west of the county. The high proportion of

spiritualities in their income - around 45 per cent as opposed to only a quarter nationally - was probably also a result of the comparative poverty of the county. In general, however, they were successful in adding to their wealth over the years. Between 1291 and 1535, their total income rose by over a third even after making allowance for Beauvale (founded in 1343). The inflation constituent of this is not easy to compute, but does not seem to effect the general conclusion of rising prosperity. For example Shelford, one of the smaller houses, had property in only a handful of parishes in 1291, a figure which had risen to 39 in 1535. Welbeck did even better and with Worksop came to rival Thurgarton. Lenton and the much smaller Blyth and Broadholm, on the other hand, seem to have failed to raise their (taxable) incomes significantly.

Table 1
Monastic income as reported in the *Taxatio* and the *Valor* (figures rounded to the nearest pound).

House	*Taxatio* (1291) value £s	*Valor* (1535) net value £s
Lenton	340	330
Thurgarton	248	259
Welbeck	112	249
Worksop	167	240
Beauvale	-	196
Rufford	118	177
Newstead	95	168
Shelford	65	117
Blyth	105	113
Wallingwells	18	58
Mattersey	52	55
Felley	11	41
Broadholm	16	16
Total	1347	2019
Average	112	155

A feature of the finances of many houses was their dependence on a major property. Thus around half of Thurgarton's income came from the ownership of the villages of Thurgarton itself and neighbouring Fiskerton; Rufford received over half from Rotherham in Yorkshire. At Blyth, though the figures varied over the years, income from the local church, market and tolls amounted to an even higher proportion. Among the smaller houses, Annesley church provided a quarter of Felley's income, while nearly all of Wallingwells' came from Carlton-in-Lindrick. Important sources of income were not always on the doorstep, however. Lenton's largest single source was the town of Bakewell, Derbyshire. The same was true of Elvaston, again in Derbyshire, for Shelford. But with the exception of Lenton, the property of Nottinghamshire houses, as with medium and smaller monasteries everywhere, was overwhelmingly confined to the county and those adjoining. Lenton, however, held lands at different times as far away as Cheshire and Buckinghamshire. But even Derbyshire property could be remote; it took a full week to bring lambs from the Peak to Lenton.

This concentration of property made for cheaper and easier management and suggests deliberate policy acting on the inevitably haphazard nature of endowment acquisitions. The cartularies point to much trading in property by the richer houses, using opportunities as they arose to rationalise their holdings. Thurgarton organised its lands into seven 'manors' on either side of the Trent, all of them within a few miles of the priory. Rufford grouped its holdings into granges under the usual Cistercian practice - 21 eventually, again mostly close to the monastery, though four were in Derbyshire. Lenton, which relied more on spiritualities than either Rufford or Thurgarton, nevertheless had large consolidated land holdings in the arable fields around it.

The actual farming regime was also adapted to make the most of natural resources. Thurgarton, like Lenton, concentrated on arable farming in its local fields, but both Lenton and Rufford used Derbyshire for sheep rearing on a large scale. Worksop cultivated liquorice in common with other farmers in the area. The evidence generally suggests that direct demesne farming continued to be practised by Nottinghamshire monasteries throughout their existence. More research is required to establish how far they moved towards becoming landlords leasing out their lands, as happened elsewhere. Some property was always let out and Lenton, to take one example, put much effort into ensuring that rents and leases were paid.

Taxable property, however, was only one source of wealth. Untaxed funds are more difficult to assess but could be very valuable. Lenton held one of England's greatest fairs every

autumn. Ostensibly it was worth only £35 in 1535, but this may have been a deliberate underestimate and seems to have taken no account of the payments in kind which the priory received from the stallholders. Worksop, too, held an important annual fair from 1296. Another monastery to benefit substantially from untaxed funds was Rufford, which in 1359 sold timber to the enormous value of £400, two or three times its annual taxable income. Beauvale and Welbeck were involved in coalmining, the former also in ironmaking, while Thurgarton's Boston property may indicate trading activity. At the other end of the scale, Beauvale received a tonne of Gascon wine and 100s annually from royal donors, while Thurgarton received a cock and a hen from each villein every Christmas, though it had to provide a festive meal for them in return.

A detail from the *Valor Ecclesiasticus,* showing a portrait of Henry VIII

For most monasteries, however, particularly the poorer ones, the great majority of their income came from the property listed in the two taxation valuations, and the fundamental importance of a house's property portfolio is indicated by the care devoted to the cartularies. A number of these still survive and their contents bears witness to the complexity of monastic finances. Thurgarton's contains over eleven hundred individual charters and other documents, Rufford's over a thousand.

Thus, in spite of some uncertainties over untaxed income, much information is available on the monasteries' sources of wealth. The evidence suggests that as far as ensuring the maximisation of their income was concerned, most

Nottinghamshire monasteries most of the time managed their affairs in a prudent and businesslike manner. Assessment of expenditure is much more difficult. At first accounting and audit systems seem to have been non-existent, and attempts by ecclesiastical authorities over many years to introduce them appear to have met with obstruction in the county as elsewhere. In the mid-thirteenth century Archbishop Gray tried to get annual audits of accounts introduced at Newstead. Well over 200 years later the 1481 Visitors to Rufford were still demanding that satisfactory systems be used to control the abbey's finances. At Newstead more drastic action was required. In the years following 1295 a succession of royal bureaucrats were appointed to manage the priory's chaotic finances.

It is therefore impossible to give any breakdown of monastic expenditure between, for example, general living expenses, hospitality, building maintenance and new construction. It is certain that few houses ever knew it themselves. Even the separation of the prior's income from that of the rest of the house, noted elsewhere in England, does not seem to have been the practice here. Both the *Taxatio* and the *Valor* list temporalities and spiritualities separately, but once received, the money or payment in kind seems to have been treated similarly whatever its source. Deductions, however, are carefully listed in the *Valor*; they include pensions, payments to ecclesiastical authorities, chantries and commuted Masses for the dead. But even these deductions are not easy to quantify, for some were taken from income before it reached the monastery, others came out of its general coffers, and the two are treated separately in the *Valor*. Some alms were also deductible for tax purposes and where allowed amounted to a few pounds a year - some £14 at Lenton, £2 6s 8d at both Shelford and Wallingwells. But some houses had no allowable alms, and it is certain that much, perhaps most, alms-giving was not tax-deductible and therefore the figures, which are typical of English monasteries generally, provide no indication of the real extent of monastic charity.

One factor affecting expenditure was the number of inmates; so it is worth comparing the figure for each house with its income (see Tables 1 and 2). Of course, neither figure was static and in some cases our information on inmate numbers is sketchy. Nevertheless, sheer physical constraints imposed a limit on numbers, and the consistency of the figures adds grounds for confidence in them. The resulting comparison shows that while inmate numbers did increase with wealth, the residents of the richest houses had much more money per head at their disposal than their poorer colleagues. Beauvale's dozen or so Carthusians seem to have been particularly well provided for, though not nearly as well as Glastonbury's 50 or so monks on an income over well over £3000.

Table 2

The approximate number of religious including the head of house in each monastery. See the chapters on individual houses for the source of these figures.

House	Approx. no. of inmates
Lenton	25
Thurgarton	20-24
Welbeck	20-26
Worksop	19 (at foundation)
Beauvale	12-14
Rufford	12 (at foundation)
Newstead	12?
Shelford	6? (2? at Dissolution)
Blyth	12+ (but only 2 in 1379)
Wallingwells	10
Mattersey	5 (at Dissolution)
Felley	3, then 5-9?
Broadholm	7-8

It is no surprise that many houses got into financial difficulties at times. Sometimes this was due to factors outside their control. Simple inadequacy of the initial endowment affected both Felley and Wallingwells for many years. At Mattersey a fire in 1279 caused damage which apparently was never fully made good. Legal expenses, then as now, could be ruinous. The Thurgarton canons put their financial difficulties early in the fourteenth century down to this. Blyth's legal expenses arose from its status as an alien house, the prior having to make repeated visits to London to plead his case, with a permanently crippling effect on its finances.

One continuing problem which affected many Nottinghamshire houses was the cost of hospitality. This was caused by the important north-south routes which passed through the county and the presence of the royal hunting grounds of Sherwood Forest. Hospitality to travellers was a Christian duty, incumbent upon religious houses through their rules to provide. But it affected some much more than others. The daily life of Worksop, indeed, seems to have been dominated at times by the demands of travellers, especially after the founding of the fair in 1296. The magnificent gatehouse actually straddled the main road and included a chapel especially provided for visitors. It became so popular a stopping-point that a rule limited stays to three days free of charge.

Worksop was one of several Nottinghamshire houses which played host to royalty. Newstead suffered particularly from this being situated conveniently in the royal hunting grounds. Kings and other important personages did not travel alone; they brought great trains of followers of both high and low estate with them, not to mention horses, all needing shelter and food according to their status. The result for Newstead as mentioned above was financial disaster for many years around 1300. Blyth, another house by a major north-south route, was also in trouble at this time from the demands of hospitality, the records making particular mention of impoverished soldiers.

Later this problem seems to have diminished, to be replaced by an even greater one. The Black Death from 1349 onwards caused enormous loss of life and disruption of all kinds. Beauvale, Blyth, Broadholm, Felley, Thurgarton, Worksop and Welbeck all claimed poverty to a greater or lesser extent in the late fourteenth and early fifteenth centuries in the aftermath of the great plague, though doubtless some claims were exaggerated. Once again the problems seem to diminish with time, though this could be due to the poorer availability of evidence on monastic life.

But some financial difficulty was of the houses' own making. Paying for grandiose building schemes or the gambling, drinking, gluttony or other vices of priors and other inmates could seriously deplete a monastery's wealth. No doubt the sudden freedom of action and access to money acquired on appointment went to the heads of some priors; others appear to have been merely incompetent administrators. At Thurgarton Prior Alexander alienated property, causing loss of income, which in turn led to the legal expenses

already noted as creditors sued for their money. But the worst example was at Welbeck, where Abbot Burton so squandered the abbey's goods over ten years around 1480 that he left it unable to celebrate Mass for lack of candles, oil and wine.

But as with morals, so with finances, it was the failures not the successes that were recorded. The fact remains that all thirteen Nottinghamshire monasteries survived until the Dissolution. Moreover, the reports of Dr Richard Layton and Dr Thomas Legh, Cromwell's Commissioners for the visitation of the monasteries in the northern province, suggest no insuperable financial difficulties at that time in spite of the problems arising from their geography - poor land and the demands of excessive hospitality. Through all the vicissitudes of 400 or so years, the religious houses continued to say the offices, provide alms, hospitality and some parish priests, and to maintain their often vast buildings. It is an achievement not to be scoffed at.

Blyth Priory

Jean Reid

The priory was founded in 1088 by Roger de Builli and his wife Muriel, and made a dependant of the Benedictine Abbey of the Holy Trinity in Rouen. It was the first post-Conquest religious house in Nottinghamshire, and was founded at a time when members of the Norman baronage were vying with one another in founding monasteries. Roger, a Norman, was a close supporter of Duke William of Normandy, now William I of England. He had been given extensive lands in Nottinghamshire, Yorkshire, and Derbyshire, including the honour of Tickhill, three miles away.

Why Roger founded a priory at Blyth is unknown, nor whether there was any existing church, but its position on the Great North Road would appear to have been a key factor. The Cartulary, thought to have been compiled mainly in the late thirteenth century, contains the Foundation Charter. This states that he gave all his manorial and judicial rights in the township of Blyth, toll and passage over a radius of about ten miles, together with demesne lands in Elton, Barnby, and Beighton (Derbyshire), and tithes of other lands in Nottinghamshire and adjourning counties. Forty shillings was to be paid annually to the abbey in Rouen. The Charter was witnessed by three priests, three officials of de Builli, and others connected with him, whose names, de Chevrecort, de Neufmarche and Deyncourt, indicate their Norman origins. These last held lands in north Nottinghamshire and surrounding areas and were important benefactors both then and later.

Roger de Builli died childless, but his family continued the connection with the priory. A nephew became a monk there, while a great great nephew founded churches at Bawtry and Austerfield, Yorkshire giving them to the priory. The family died out in 1235. Confirmation charters were given by Henry I and subsequent kings. That given by Henry II was attested by Archbishop Thomas Becket, when Chancellor, at the 'Castle of Blyth' - the name given to the castle of Tickhill when used for royal and administrative purposes. The priory's future history would be influenced by three significant factors: its geographical position - it lay at the junction of important roads, north and south (the Via Regia), with crossings of two small rivers east and west; the ownership of the church and township of Blyth; and its 'alien' status.

Architectural History

All that remains today of the former priory is the present parish church. The nave of the conventual church with its side aisles was in effect the parish church before the Dissolution and so it continued, while the chancel end of the monks and the other conventual buildings were in due course destroyed. Pevsner points out that the nave, north aisle, and north and south arcades of the church date stylistically from probably no later than 1100 and thus indicate that, contrary to normal practice, the nave was likely to have been built before the chancel. The only decorative features on the plain rounded arcades are the capitals of uncertain motif, though some hold crudely carved faces. Two linked faces in the north aisle are

Two linked faces on the capital of a north aisle pillar

traditionally seen as those of the founder and his wife, though there is no clear evidence for this supposition. The large undivided openings of the triforium, with obvious similarities to those of St Etienne at Caen, show the influence of the Romanesque architecture of Normandy. The clerestory over the south arcade is of later construction, as evidenced by the slender columns and the pure cushion capitals of a more advanced Norman style. The clerestory windows over the north arcade were replaced post-Dissolution. Originally the piers would have reached to a high wooden roof, but were reduced around 1230 to provide the springing for the ribs of the stone vaulting of a new roof. The bosses are also thirteenth-century. Unusually, the cloisters were on the north side of the church. Excavations have indicated that the monks built an apsidal-ended chancel with two straight-ended chapels and that the transepts had apsidal chapels at their eastern ends. All that can be seen today is the high plain Norman chancel arch visible only from the outside.

The increasing independence and demands of the parish led to the destruction of the Norman south aisle and to its widening to the full width of the south transept. This provided the parish with its own chancel and rood screen. Work started about 1290 and, while the Norman arcade was retained, a new south wall with five pointed-arch windows was built. What was probably the former south doorway with its Early English outer arch was moved to its present position. The present west tower was begun before 1400 and was the responsibility of the parish. This used the space of the westernmost bays of the nave but there are the remains of two small spiral stairways at its foot which would have been part of the original west end.

Rare eleventh-century painted scrollwork on a capital

The church today is important for its painted decoration. The first painting, dating to the earliest building, is the very late eleventh-century scrollwork on the capital of the easternmost pier to the left of the present altar. Such early painting is almost unique in this country. With cleaning it would be possible to see the thirteenth-century paintwork on the vaulting and the bosses. Later painting dates to the period of the parish church's 'independence'.

South aisle arcade showing the influence of Romanesque architecture

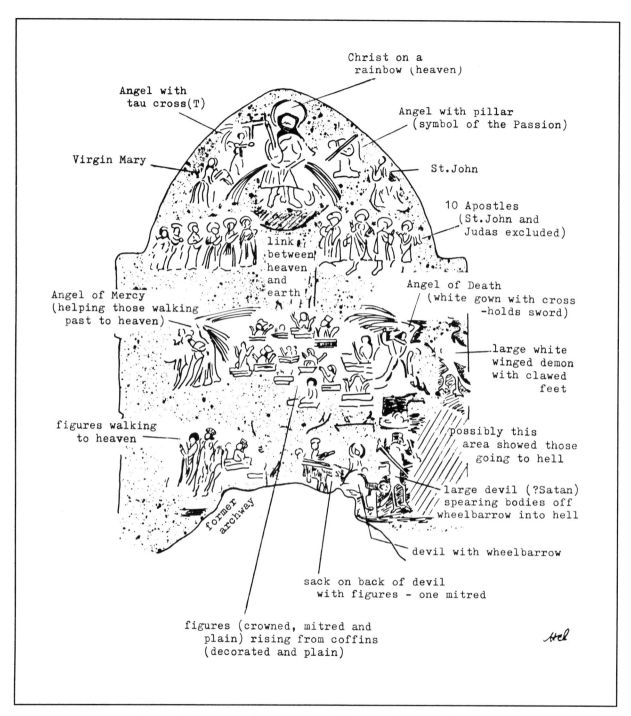

Christ on a
rainbow (heaven)

Angel with
tau cross(T)

Angel with pillar
(symbol of the Passion)

Virgin Mary

St.John

10 Apostles
(St.John and
Judas excluded)

link
between
heaven
and
earth

Angel of Mercy
(helping those walking
past to heaven)

Angel of Death
(white gown with cross
-holds sword)

large white
winged demon
with clawed
feet

figures walking
to heaven

possibly this
area showed those
going to hell

large devil (?Satan)
spearing bodies off
wheelbarrow into hell

former
archway

devil with wheelbarrow

sack on back of devil
with figures - one mitred

figures (crowned, mitred and
plain) rising from coffins
(decorated and plain)

A diagram of the Doom painting with a suggested interpretation by Hirst Conservation

In the late fifteenth century the delicate vaulted rood screen was erected and the panel paintings of the same period probably inserted. These are interesting for their iconography as can be seen below.

> **Table 3**
> The paintings on the nine panels of the rood screen
>
> 1-3 Blank
>
> 4 St Stephen: holds three stones, stone on head (he was stoned to death).
>
> 5 St Agatha: sword through breast (her breasts were cut off).
>
> 6 St Edmund: crowned and sceptred, holding three arrows (he was king of the East Angles, shot by arrows, then beheaded).
>
> 7 St Helen: crowned and carrying a tau cross (legend says that she discovered the cross on which Christ was crucified).
>
> 8 St Barbara: with palm (symbol of victory) and tower (she was imprisoned in a tower).
>
> 9 St Ursula: protecting her virgins (legend says that she died in a massacre following a pilgrimage).

There are earlier but unidentifiable paintings on the nearby nave screen. Of great importance, though again probably the responsibility of the parish and not the monks, is the fifteenth-century Doom painting on the east wall. This wall was probably built at the end of the fourteenth century and where the former chancel screen would have been. It is a further symbol of the division between priory and parish. At the Reformation this painting, so much part of the iconography of the medieval Catholic church, was covered with lime wash. It was cleaned and restored in 1988 to coincide with the nine hundredth anniversary of the priory's foundation.

Economic History

To the foundation grants were added lands of varying extent by descendants of the founder and by new local landowners such as the de Styrrups and the de Cresseys. In the twelfth and thirteenth centuries the priory's main sources of income were from 23 places in Nottinghamshire, ten in Yorkshire, and nine elsewhere; it also acquired numerous smallholdings at this time. The circumstances of some of the transfers recorded in the Cartulary tells us as much about the donors' relationship with the priory as the intricacies of its finances. For example, in the late twelfth or early thirteenth century Brother Peter was received as a monk having given timber and a toft; one Mathilda gave land and as a benefactor was received into an honorary sisterhood; Robert Rascald quitclaimed 40 acres in return for a corrody for life, a robe or 5s annually, and 40s; and Roger, son of Reinald the chamberlain, gave land and rent in return for the office of gatekeeper. The most poignant gifts are the many grants of land made by poverty-stricken peasantry in return for money and clothes 'in my great necessity'.

The taxable income given in the 1291 *Taxatio* shows spiritualities totalling £69, including £50 for the church of Blyth. Temporalities in Nottinghamshire were £44. When the priory was assessed as an alien house in 1379, however, there was a considerable overall increase. The church at Blyth was now valued at £66 and income from toll, market, pleas, and perquisites of court on market days amounted to £60 a year, indicating how important the founder's bequest was to the priory's finances.

Hospitality was a considerable financial drain. Visitors including heads of other houses, came, for example, to witness agreements or to give support when the notorious Blyth tournament was to be banned. There were probably also those unable to stay at the nearby castle at Tickhill when royal writs were being issued there. And there were merchants, pilgrims, and soldiers in transit. In 1249 an annual pension from the church at Weston was allocated to help with the cost of hospitality. In 1379 the prior was assessed as needing £10 a year for this. In 1308 the abbot in Rouen was asked not to send more monks to the priory was already already impoverished by soldiers stopping on their way to the Scottish wars, Blyth being one of the assembly points.

Disputes over tithes were on-going. One of the most serious was with the vicar of Blyth. Agreement was finally reached in 1287, recognising the tithes and offerings due to each party, but also the responsibilities they incurred.

The vicar was to serve both the church of Blyth and those of Bawtry and Austerfield; he also had the right to sit suitably vested in the choir on 24 feast days, to eat then with the monks and to have other perquisites. The dispute, however, rumbled on; but in 1534 the vicar still had his house and toft, his 20s pension, a quarter of rye a year and other benefits as listed in 1287. Another long-standing dispute over tithes was with the founder's gift of the church at Laughton in Yorkshire, also settled in 1287, with the intervention of the Archbishop of York.

At the beginning of the fourteenth century there were indications of growing impoverishment. In 1310 the Archbishop decreed that because of debts no new monks should be admitted. In 1314 permission was given to sell the tithes of Bawtry and Austerfield for three years and the tolls of Blyth for two years. Visitation records continue citing dilapidations and debts.

During the Hundred Years War with France, Blyth was particularly vulnerable because, as an alien priory, it was seen as a security risk. The prior was alternately saddled with a royal nominee to oversee the economy, fined in order to regain custody, or back in control in periods of peace. All this had a cumulatively deleterious effect. In 1348 the manor of Elton was leased out 'because of great charges in defence of the rights of his priory taken into (the king's) hands'[1] and rented back. In 1388 'divers wastes, dilapidations have been committed ... divine services, hospitalities discontinued ... and (the prior) has assaulted the king's physician while farmer (overseer)'.[2] That these overseers were not efficient is illustrated nine years later when the same man, back in Blyth, was given a royal pardon for monies due. A similar crisis is described in the Patent Rolls of 1421. An added burden was that as head of an alien house, the prior had to travel to London to plead his case. For this and other journeyings he was allowed £16 in the 1379 assessment.

How much of the economic decline was due to inefficient management, the demands of hospitality, the effects of being an alien priory, or changes in land management is difficult to determine. But this decline was already recognised in 1319 when the priory's assessment for its contribution for the Scottish war was a third of that of the

houses of Mattersey and Newstead. This was confirmed by the many entries in the Fine Rolls in the fifteenth century excusing Blyth of all or part of the tenths 'because of notorious poverty'.

In the *Valor Ecclesiasticus* the priory's total gross income is given as £125, spiritualities being £60, temporalities £66. The rectory of Blyth was now valued at £44, but there is no explanation for the dramatic decrease in the value of tolls and other dues for the township to £2 from the 1379 figure of £60. The net value of the priory in 1535 was £112. From being the fourth wealthiest house in Nottinghamshire in 1291, Blyth had now sunk to the seventh.

Monastic Life

The life of the priory was as much involved with secular matters as religious. The priory exercised feudal rights over a small but active community covering varying occupations: amongst these were William Aurifaber (goldsmith), Reginald Sissor (tailor) and Thomas Becarious (shepherd). The correct procedure for the weekly market and annual fair had to be followed and taxes and tolls levied. The latter often led to disputes, some of considerable importance, such as that with the citizens of Lincoln in 1291 with damages of £1,000 involved. Judicial rights were jealously protected; in the late thirteenth century a man captured in Blyth market place on suspicion of theft was taken to Tickhill. The prior claimed trial in his court. The Tickhill gatekeeper demanded payment, but was overruled, and the prisoner returned to Blyth. The prior was also responsible for the erection and use of a gallows, a responsibility confirmed not for the first time as late as 1411. In 1194 Blyth was one of seven places licensed by Richard I for the holding of tournaments. Seen as a potential source of disorder, however, these were frequently banned by the Crown, which made the prior responsible for enforcing such bans.

The number of monks was not large. At the end of the thirteenth century there were at least twelve, plus the prior. A hundred years later during the French wars after the expulsion order of 1377 when the French monks had to leave, there were only two. But by then the priory had other inhabitants. A list of 1379 gives a picture of the conventual community: the former prior 'in his old age', his servant, two chaplains, three clerks, a steward, a sergeant at arms, nine persons receiving corrodies, a cook, a baker, two servants, and the prior's groom ... a picture of the monastery as an old people's home.

The priors were either French or English and of varying calibre. William Burdon, prior from 1273 to 1303, left his stamp. The cartulary appears to have been started under him. In it numerous documents attest to his involvement in land and other settlements, including the agreement leading to the more formal division between priory and parish, as well as that following the acrimonious dispute with the citizens of Lincoln. Prior William also ordered a survey of the priory's properties and tenants. In contrast there was Prior Thomas de Vymond who in 1373 with many followers broke into the park of William de Furnival in Sheffield and 'hunted, felled his trees, fished in his free fishery, dug in his quarry ... carried away stones and coal ... deer ... hares, conies ... and assaulted his men and servants'.[3] Visitation records were, of course, more concerned with correcting defects than giving praise. Thus in 1307 the Archbishop details how the convent should be run: the prior should exercise control more effectively ... should be with the monks in the dorter ... no taunts to be made against anyone ... a cellarer and almoner should be appointed. The implication here is there was a lack of firm religious and financial control.

There were both French and English monks at Blyth, but it was not a popular posting for the French. Norman monks were frequently sent back to Rouen because of disruptive behaviour and the abbot was requested to send only monks of whose religiosity he was confident. Archbishop Romeyn wrote to the Abbot in Rouen in 1291 asking him not to keep his monks at Blyth more than four to five years since it was regarded as a place of exile. Archbishop Greenfield repeated this gloomy request in 1310. As an alien priory the French abbot was ostensibly in control, but the Archbishop exercised influence not only through his visitations, but also through a running correspondence with the abbot. On the other hand, also in 1291, Archbishop Romeyn protested against the recall of a monk, Nicholas de Bretteville, and of the possible recall of William Burdon, 'our dear son', both being considered of great value to the priory. The former was later to become prior following the

Archbishop's recommendation and would finally end his days being cared for in the priory, having resigned because of old age and paralysis. In 1289 a request was made for a French monk to return to France as the climate did not agree with him. This was obviously not acceded to, because two years later he was sent back because of 'intolerable behaviour'.

The wars with France taxed the patience and energies of the priors. They had to cope with royal suspicion and demands, and were frequently called to London where they pleaded to be left alone. Having its own seal, the priory was fortunate in being able to show some independence of Rouen. One prior is recorded in 1387 as lying in the Fleet Prison awaiting 'to be called in Chancery', to answer for the disastrous state of his house during the war. Being an alien priory affected not only the economy and morale, but also the management of the priory. The King assumed the right of appointment to benefices belonging to the priory during periods of war with France. When Prior English died in 1409, the King appointed the next prior, and this function never returned to Rouen but remained with the King until the Dissolution.

The Dissolution

There are few records of the fifteenth century concerning the priory, and one can only imagine the feelings of the monks as they saw the secular side of their church going from strength to strength. When the commissioners visited in 1536 they reported four cases of serious sexual offences and one of adultery. But in all the previous visitation records there appears to be only one reference to such offences, in 1315. In 1536 Prior Dalton wrote to Cromwell that he was sick and could not come to London to present his case. He was given a small pension of twenty marks on the final dissolution of his house. Nothing is known of the arrangements for the other monks, nor for those who might have been receiving corrodies, nor for any other inhabitants of this ancient house.

Later History

After the Dissolution the priory and rectory were leased to Sir Gervase Clifton of nearby Hodsock, whose family had been influential in the building of the west tower over a century earlier. It then passed through various hands until in 1635 it was bought by John Mellish of London, a merchant tailor. In 1684 his son pulled down the hall known as Blyth Abbey, which stood on the site of some of the conventual buildings, in order to rebuild. Completing the destruction of the church's east end, the choir, transepts and central tower, he appropriated the last bays in the north aisle and nave and built a family vault under the latter. He also built the gabled façade over the old Norman chancel arch.

In the later eighteenth century William Mellish created a park and pleasure garden. This not only obliterated any possible remaining evidence of the priory buildings but significantly altered the lie of the land. It lowered the ground levels to the north and east of the church, so the ground at the east end dropped suddenly into what is now the garden of a modern house whose name, Centry Garth, indicates the likely place of the monks' cemetery.

Much of the estate was bought by Josiah Walker of Masborough Iron Works, Yorkshire, in the early nineteenth century. His family resisted all development. The railway never came, Bawtry became the local market town and Blyth retired into an attractive backwater now by-passed by the A1. Blyth Hall was pulled down in 1972 to be replaced by a number of private houses. Today all that remains of Nottinghamshire's only Benedictine religious house is the church. This is normally open every day. The patronage lies with Trinity College, Cambridge, to whom it was given on its foundation in 1546 by Henry VIII.

References

1. *Calendar of Patent Rolls, 1348-50*, 46
2. *Ibid., 1385-9*, 553
3. *Ibid., 1370-4*, 390

Access

OS SK 624 873. Blyth lies off the A1 south of Bawtry: take A614, signposted to Blyth, about 4 miles north of Ranby. The church is in the centre of the village.

Blyth Priory in its rural setting

Worksop Priory

Joy Bristow

 orksop is a market town situated near Sherwood Forest in north-west Nottinghamshire, close to the Great North Road. The priory was built on the site of a small Norman church at the village of Radford and at the time of its foundation was to the east of the town, near the river Ryton. It has impressive twin western towers and a disappointing modern spire and lies close to the present town centre. The fee of Worksop was granted by William the Conqueror to Roger de Builli, and by marriage passed to William de Lovetot, who in March 1103 gave it to the Augustinian Order to found a monastery. The fee included the manor of Worksop, with its meadows and mills, and the lands and tithes of several churches, including Gringley and Walkeringham. The canons were to have 'the use and profit of the produce' of these. The first eighteen canons and a prior are believed to have come from Huntingdon. The priory church was originally dedicated to St Cuthbert, but in the time of the founder's son, Richard, it was dedicated additionally to the Virgin Mary. Changes of patrons occurred through marriage, first to the Furnivals, then to Sir Thomas Nevil, High Treasurer of England. In the fifteenth century the patronage passed to John Talbot, who became the Earl of Shrewsbury, and this family was still the patron at the Dissolution.

Architectural History

The original endowment included the small Norman parish church, which may have been rebuilt or redesigned for the use of the canons. Later a monastic choir with possibly three apses was built. Then in 1140 the first bay of the present nave was commenced. The first pair of pillars may indicate the limit of the parish church, with perhaps a rood-screen or loft above. The nave was 140 feet long and 60 feet wide externally, with unbroken aisle-arcades supported by pillars, with a range of triforium arches above. The nine bays of the arcade, dating from c.1170, are impressive, the piers alternately round and octagonal and decorated with nailhead, simple leaf and dog-tooth carving. The area of the central tower, together with the transepts, occupied 100 feet from north to south and may have formed the ante-church of the conventual choir.

Around 1200 the original choir was replaced by one in the Early English style; and in 1240-50 the striking Lady Chapel was built by the order of Richard de Lovetot's daughter, Maude Furnival. It was attached to the eastern end of the south transept and to the western portion of the south aisle wall and contained fine lancet windows. The ambry, double *piscina* and *sedilia* are still in a good state of preservation.

The inner door of the south porch

The inner south porch door, believed to be one of the oldest in England, is original and was made in the thirteenth century of yew from Sherwood Forest. It is decorated with

The nave with its impressive Romanesque capitals

floriated ironwork. On the side door jambs can be seen small Jerusalem crosses which are said to have been made as a votive offering by crusaders, carving the first part of the cross prior to departing and finishing the cross on their return. Maude's husband, Sir Gerald de Furnival, died in Jerusalem in 1219. Later, when her elder son Thomas also died on crusade, she insisted on his brother Gerard travelling to the Holy Land to bring back his heart for burial at Worksop.

As at Blyth, the cloisters were on the north side of the church. The wall running northwards retains an entrance doorway and several windows of the *cellarium,* above which would have been a dormitory. When a nearby school was built, many animal bones, boars' tusks and parts of deer horns were found, suggesting that this area may have been the kitchen of the monastery. The refectory and warming house were also probably in the northern range of these buildings. The reredorter would be near to running

water, where there is evidence of a ditch. A well was discovered in the centre of the cloister garth, and evidence for the Chapter House was found on the eastern side of the site. Situated to the south-east of the area was the canons' cemetery, to the west of the priory. The fishponds were located at a point where later maps show a field called 'Great Pond Yard'.

The common practice was to build monastic infirmaries away from the main buildings. During excavations in the nineteenth century an area with edging stones was uncovered, thought to be the hearth of the infirmary, placed centrally, the smoke escaping through a louvre in the roof. The infirmary would have been a hall-like building with the beds arranged around the sides.

The Gatehouse was built in the early fourteenth century, permission being granted by the Archbishop of York in 1314 to fell 200 oaks for its construction. The chapel and

The early fourteenth century gatehouse

stone mullioned windows at each end, with quatrefoil tracery at the south window. The cell of the brother guestmaster leads off this room. The chapel and shrine are unusual and well preserved features. The porch has doors on either side, to assist the movement of people, and a beautifully decorated ceiling. From the shrine, stone steps lead up to a chapel dedicated to the Virgin Mary. The *piscinas* by the altar are original. It seems likely that travellers and pilgrims used the chapel to give thanks for the food and shelter they had received and to venerate an image of the Virgin which stood in the shrine.

Economic History

The priory was fortunate in its founding family, the de Lovetots, who continued to add to the original endowment in each generation. In a charter of 1130 William de Lovetot made a further grant of chapel furniture, the tithes of his seven churches in the honour of Blyth, a portion of the church at Treswell and all the lands and rights belonging to it, which included pannage, venison, fish and other commodities. This charter was confirmed by his son Richard, who added valuable gifts of his own, including land in Hardwick, the site of Worksop town and numerous houses and meadows. Land was also acquired in other ways. Edward I granted the priory 60 acres in Rumwood (whose location has not been identified) at a rental of 10s, to enclose and cultivate as it wished. In fact, the canons enclosed an extra thirteen acres, which led to their being asked for more rent. In the event, in 1335 Edward III, on appeal to him and wishing to show favour in return for the expenses the priory had incurred on his visits, granted it the whole acreage rent-free for ever.

As a result of these gifts, Worksop was always moderately well provided for. In 1291 its taxable income amounted to £167, making it the third wealthiest house in the county, though this was only half that of Lenton. At that time it relied on spiritualities to a greater extent than any other Nottinghamshire monastery, with nearly three-quarters of income arising from these sources. But so successful was it in increasing its 'temporal' income, however, that by the Dissolution this almost matched that from 'spiritual' sources. Its gross income rose to over £300, nearly three-quarters of Lenton's.

shrine on the south-east corner were added later in the century. The need for a building to accommodate travellers perhaps arose from the granting of a market and fair to Thomas Furnival in 1296. The market cross, though not now in its original position was also erected as a result of this. The ground floor of the gatehouse, with small rooms on either side, is divided by what was originally a public road, not diverted until the 1890s. The ceiling of the archway has the original timbers, and a stone staircase of the early fifteenth century leads to the upper room. Originally this was reached by a staircase on the outside of the north-east corner. It runs the length of the building, and was the Guest Chamber where hospitality was given to travellers, who were allowed to stay for three days before any questions were asked. The Guest Chamber has a splendid oak-beamed ceiling, a large open fireplace and

The initial endowment included lands, mills, fishponds, tithes and rents from Normandy as well as from England. The canons were allowed to collect waggon-loads of wood from the forest for building; they also had privileges of fodder for their animals. The priory was situated on forest soils and had extensive pasture spreading over hundreds of acres for sheep-rearing, which was the community's main economic activity. Thirty acres of arable were held in demesne, together with 150 acres of pasture and 200 of open ground for the growing of crops. These normal agricultural activities were undertaken for the canons by servants and lay brethren. In addition, the canons cultivated liquorice. This perennial herb, which had roots up to one metre long and one centimetre thick, was used as a sweetener in cooking, and as an effective mask for the taste of medicines such as cough mixtures, syrups and elixirs. Liquorice continued to be cultivated in Worksop until the late eighteenth century.

Royal visitors came to Nottinghamshire and especially the monasteries in Sherwood Forest for the hunting, and the visits of Edward I and Edward III have already been mentioned. Lesser folk perhaps started to come to Worksop in numbers as a result of the granting of the market and annual fair in 1296, with the magnificent gatehouse being built, in part, to provide for them. Initially the priory seems to have profited from this influx because in 1347 it was able to lend the King over £5 towards the cost of the war in France, to be repaid next All Saints Day. But in 1408 and 1409 the prior and canons pleaded poverty and asked to be granted exemption from taxation because of the numerous travellers provided with hospitality. Travellers seem to have begun to abuse the priory's generosity and were limited to a three-day stay.

There were also other demands on the priory's resources. The priory was, of course, obliged to give alms. The daily

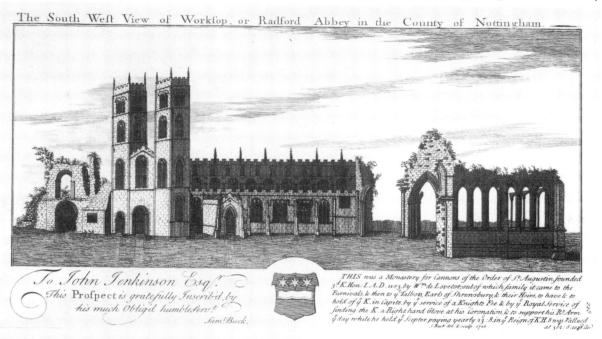

Samuel Buck's engraving of the south west view of Worksop Priory, 1726

Another important activity at Worksop was accommodating travellers. It was part of the Christian duty of monasteries to provide this and rich and poor alike availed themselves of it. But its impact varied greatly between the houses.

dishes of food for the poor, together with the Lady Dish (given annually on Lady Day), cost the priory £10 a year. At Christmas a 'pittance' was provided in memory of the founder, William de Lovetot. This consisted of wheat, rye, bread and beer and cost another £10. Numerous corrodians, too, had to be cared for in later life, under terms they had arranged earlier with the canons.

Monastic Life

Worksop was a religious house of medium size and the canons' days were spent in prayer and services, but they also worked in the *scriptorium,* writing manuscripts and books, mostly for the use of the community. Little is known of the history of manuscript illumination at Worksop, but in 1896 a Bestiary containing 106 miniatures was offered for sale in Germany. It was bought by William Morris, who found both the writing and miniatures superior to anything held by the British Museum. A note in the book stated that it had been given to Worksop Priory in 1187 by Philip, canon of Lincoln, together with other books. Perhaps this inspired the canons of Worksop to start illumination themselves.

The most important manuscript known from Worksop is the Tickhill Psalter, attributed to John Tickhill, who was prior between 1303 and 1313 when he was deposed for incontinence and dilapidation. The beautifully illustrated manuscript, with the text written on vellum, comprises nineteen regular quires of eight folios each. The 482 miniatures illustrate portions of the Old Testament, the greater number showing the life of David. They form perhaps the longest continuous series of Biblical scenes in a Gothic manuscript. This remarkable Psalter is now in the New York Library, but a replica is held in Worksop Library.

Further evidence of the intellectual life of the priory is provided by the work of a canon named Pigot, who in the fourteenth century, wrote an historical rhyme which speaks of the foundation of the priory and describes the Lords of Worksop, their gifts and their places of burial:

Which had that affiaunce and inspiration
The monastery of Worssoppe first for to found,
Mortest therto goods thereupon,
Wooddes, medues and moundes: to say a greate grounde,
Therefore in speciall, certs we are bounde
pray for his soule, and his successours,
As we nightly do, and dayly at all houres.[1]

The priory had a great number of churches in its care, including the church at Sheffield, now the Cathedral, and it provided spiritual oversight to a parish sometimes permanently, sometimes until a permanent vicar was appointed. The foundation in 1156 of Felley Priory from Worksop is an indication of the early success of Worksop. Felley remained subject to it for 100 years. The priors also had secular duties. One was ordered by the King to go to Blyth in 1251 to stop the tournament, accompanied by the Prior of Lenton. The Visitation reports throw some light on daily life. In 1280 the prior was ordered not to allow anyone to hold private property, and all lockers were to be searched four times a year. Also the canons were not to go outside the gates unnecessarily. Two canons had to be brought back from a grange and were ordered to remain within the walls because of misconduct. Servants, too, could get into trouble. Some were brought before the courts in 1370, 1374 and 1393 for causing deaths, but all received pardons.

The Dissolution

The priory was surrendered on 15 November 1538 after existing for 436 years under nineteen priors, the last being Thomas Stokes. It had been visited by Legh and Layton who found four canons guilty of unnatural sin, and one desiring release from his vows. The priory had an income of £240 net and debts of 200 marks. Just prior to dissolution, the canons sold many animals and grain, but it is not known who benefited from this sale. The valuable plate listed at the Dissolution included a pair of silver candlesticks; a censor of silver; a ship of silver; five chalices; two cups with gilt covers; two salts and one cover; twelve silver spoons and four ale cups. In a letter to Cromwell dated 1538 Sir George Lawson stated he had 'already committed the custody of them to substantial persons and have sold none'.

On surrendering the convent Thomas Stokes received a pension of £50, and the other fifteen canons received ones varying from £6 to 40s. These were due to be paid at Pentecost and Martinmas, but were always in arrears; and stoppages were also deducted. A small number of the canons sold their pensions for a cash settlement. The so-called Jesus House, close to the priory, as well as the farm of the vicarage were later granted to Prior Stokes.

Later History

In November 1541 the priory and its lands were granted to Francis Talbot, Earl of Shrewsbury, in exchange for Farnham Royal in Buckinghamshire. Francis agreed to this exchange, but with the manor of Farnham Royal went the honour of providing a glove at the coronation. This honour he was not willing to lose, so Henry VIII agreed it should pass to the lords of the manor of Worksop. The glove, richly embroidered, was for the right hand of the sovereign, and was to be placed on the hand prior to receiving the sceptre. The lands of the priory were held by the Shrewsbury family until the seventeenth century when they passed by marriage to the Duke of Norfolk, and in 1840 were sold to the Duke of Newcastle.

After the Dissolution, the east end of the large church and most of the monastic buildings were destroyed, and the lead and timbers from the roof taken away. The nave being the parochial portion of the church was spared, although arches and aisles were walled up and it appears to have fallen into disrepair. Repair work started in the seventeenth century, converting the triforium arches into windows. In the 1800s restoration recommenced. The aisle arcades were out of line, one by fifteen inches, but were restored by the provision of new bases. Old aisles were rebuilt, doorways reopened, windows inserted, and the church was reroofed, reseated and repaved. Work continued into the twentieth century with the new east end and central tower being built in the 1970s.

Since the Dissolution the gatehouse has had many uses. In 1628 it was used as an elementary school and in the early nineteenth century was a school for poor children. Until recently it was used as an art gallery and tea room.

References

1. W. Dugdale, *Monasticon Anglicanum,* vol. vi (London, 1830), 122

Access

OS SK 585795. Worksop is situated in north Nottinghamshire off the A57. The Gatehouse is on Potter Street. The Priory is on Priorswell Road and there is a car park adjoining. The Priory is open during church services, or by arrangement.

Lenton Priory

Janet Jones and Sheila Chambers

Lenton Priory was founded in the reign of Henry I by William Peveril. The foundation date is generally accepted as 1108, at which time Peveril was custodian of Nottingham Castle and in possession of a good deal of local land. The foundations of the priory were laid within sight of the castle in an elbow of the river Leen, newly diverted by Peveril to provide the castle with water and a means of transport for supplies. Peveril dedicated the house to the Holy Trinity of God and gave it to Pontius, Abbot of Cluny, and his successors. At this time Peveril agreed an annual fee of one mark of silver to Cluny as the mother house. The foundation was in the names of William I, William II and Henry I and their respective Queens, and for the good of Peveril's own soul and that of his wife and children.

The position of the building adjacent to the River Leen provided usefully for dispersal of both sewage and kitchen refuse. It stood on fertile ground, away from the flood plain of the river Trent and convenient for the tracks running west to east and north to south. The west-east track ran from Stapleford through Beeston, following the path of Cut Through Lane, past Keighton village and on to Nottingham Castle. The north-south track ran out of Sherwood Forest southward, roughly along the line of Gregory Street and on to the river Trent at Wilford. These busy roads would have been used for passage to the castle and town of Nottingham and fording the river. The route leading to the river-crossing and another west of the Leen, used for transporting coal from Wollaton to the south side of the river, were eventually controlled by the priors of Lenton, who secured the routes with chains and required all travellers to purchase a license to use them.

Peveril endowed the priory with the township of Lenton, including seven mills, and also the townships of Radford, Morton and Keighton. Morton and Keighton no longer exist but were then small settlements close to the site of the priory. Woods and 'plains' in both Newthorpe and Papplewick were also included in the endowment. Henry I gave consent for the three churches of Nottingham, St Mary, St Peter and St Nicholas, and the churches of Radford and Langar to be given to the priory, together with the tithes of fisheries in Nottinghamshire. The tithes of Bakewell were also granted, together with other tithes in Derbyshire, including some from stud farms, from lead and from venison. All of these Derbyshire spiritualities came from land originally bestowed upon William Peveril by Henry I.

Thus Lenton began its existence with endowments greater than any other monastery in Nottinghamshire. It became a religious house of considerable importance, having much influence throughout the county and beyond. The physical size of the buildings was an obvious indicator of the priory's status. The number of monks averaged about 25 and rarely exceeded 30, with an unknown number of lay brethren.

Architectural History

The immense physical structure of Lenton Priory, which once dominated the area, is now only indicated by a few scant remains. Its great size, similar to that of Southwell Minster, is suggested by our knowledge of other Cluniac houses and the evidence from several excavations carried out this century. The earlier eighteenth century excavations by William Stretton did not provide overall dimensions, but did unearth many interesting artefacts. The most significant of these is the beautifully carved Norman font. Numerous decorative tiles were also discovered when Stretton dug the foundations of his own house on site. The tiles were probably produced at Lenton by peripatetic craftsmen, for similarly stamped tiles have been found at other Midland sites.

Excavations carried out in the twentieth century have greatly increased the evidence for the monastic buildings. The pillar base which remains *in situ* on Priory Street is of circular construction in Derbyshire millstone grit, the centre void being filled with local stone and shale. There were originally twelve of these pillars supporting the chancel of the church, while the nave was supported by further huge compound pillars. These circular pillars may have been similar in size and decoration to those in Durham Cathedral. Much of the building stone seems to have come from Stanton in Derbyshire and more locally from Bulwell, both sources for stone used in the building of Nottingham castle. An important find of the excavations in the 1960s was the foundation of the *pulpitum* with an adjacent altar on the western side. The *pulpitum* was the stone screen which separated the chancel from the nave, and the existence of an altar within the nave seems to indicate use of this area for parochial worship.

Encaustic floor tiles from Lenton Priory

The cloisters were probably located to the south of the church in conformity with the usual monastic pattern, enabling the reredorter, or privy, to be placed near or astride the river Leen. The cloister is unlikely to have been on the north side of the conventual church, since this ground was used for burials from the church of St Anthony, the parish church of Lenton prior to 1842 (when the present Victorian church was opened). Little on site evidence remains of what must have been an immense complex. The foundations of an infirmary lie beneath St Anthony's church near to the site of the priory gatehouse, and those of a lady chapel adjoin the apsidal end of the conventual church.

Much building at Lenton was done during the first half of the thirteenth century, when Henry III provided many grants of timber and licences for quarrying in Sherwood Forest. This was an era of new building, rebuilding and repair, with quarrying rights in 1229 assisting specifically in the rebuilding of the collapsed tower. Much of the timber granted was for roofing material, used in the dormitory in 1229, the refectory in 1231, repairs of the infirmary roof in 1236, and in 1244 for the 'making of the chapter house'. Many more timber grants were made during the thirteenth century, one being for 32 oaks from Sherwood Forest. Construction of the prior's chamber in 1256 is confirmed by a further stone quarrying grant for this purpose and probably indicates the culmination of the building programme. Workshops and outbuildings were probably then added as needed, whilst repair work was continuous.

Economic History

Lenton was the richest Nottinghamshire monastery from the start and it remained so until the Dissolution. In 1291 its taxable income amounted to £330, thirty times as much as Felley, the poorest house, and a quarter of all the county's monastic income. Nevertheless, in comparison with other houses, it does not seem to have managed its wealth well. One of the problems was that it relied somewhat heavily on spiritualities, which accounted for more than half its income. Major sources included St Mary's church, Nottingham, the tithes of Langar and the church of Lenton, part of Peveril's original endowment. Its property was also very widely spread and arose from no fewer than six counties, with contributions coming from as far afield as Bedfordshire and Buckinghamshire. Amounts varied from £66 from Bakewell (much more even than St Mary's, Nottingham) to 1s 8d from Rempstone.

Tithes, in particular, were difficult to collect, the small ones being hardly worth the effort required. There was thus continual buying and selling of tithes in the attempt to make them profitable. But this scarcely consolidated them, for in 1534 the priory still had spiritual income from seven counties, contributions from Cheshire and Yorkshire having

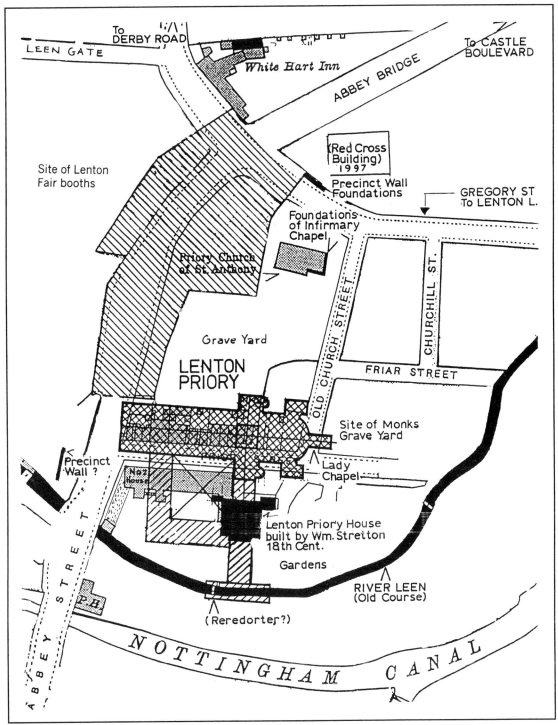

Plan of the priory complex based on the 1938 OS map relating the medieval plan to the present day road plan

come to replace those from the two Home Counties. Moreover, unlike most other of the county's larger monasteries, Lenton's dependence on spiritualities increased rather than decreased over the years. This is not to suggest that the priory was short of temporal income. Initially this exceeded all other Nottinghamshire houses except Thurgarton. The monks put in much effort to ensure that rents were paid: disputes with tenants were frequent, and many fines for rents not paid promptly were recorded.

But in the temporal sphere Lenton's property was equally well scattered, and the priory had important holdings in the Peak District. This wide spread made management difficult and expensive. In 1297 it took seven days for a monk and eight servants to drive lambs from the Peak to Lenton. The priory does not seem to have amalgamated its estates into manageable groups, as did other large monasteries. Nor was it successful in adding to its early endowments. Most of its property was acquired early in the life of the priory, with so few later additions that at the Dissolution, though still the county's wealthiest house, it accounted for only a sixth of the overall monastic income. One result of its many endowments was the obligation to care for corrodians, who had given money or land for their support. In 1324 there were no fewer than twenty pensioners of various types living at Lenton, some with additional servants, compared to an almost equal number of monks.

Lenton's endowment included a large acreage of demesne on the fertile land around the priory. In 1300 the area sown with crops was 400 acres. Whether this represented half or two-thirds of the arable land available is uncertain; the crop rotation could have been biennial or triennial. Unfortunately our knowledge of the administration of the demesne is limited by the poor quality of the surviving accounts and the many gaps in them. We do know, however, that in 1296-7 the crops sown were wheat, rye, oats, barley and peas. Sheep farming was also important to the priory demesne.

Perhaps even more important was the great Lenton Fair. Granted by Henry II probably in 1164, it originally lasted eight days - increasing to twelve days by a charter of Henry III. Commencing on St Martin's Day (11 November), traditionally a time of feasting and drinking, the date was doubtless chosen by the monks so that they could sell their harvest and livestock surpluses. For nearly 300 years it was one of the largest fairs in the country. The prior obtained the monopoly of the fair, and no market was allowed in Nottingham, whilst the Lenton fair was in progress. This caused loss of trade to the town and forced the people of Nottingham to go to Lenton to buy their provisions. The priory also received toll money from visitors to the town. Not surprisingly these privileges led to disputes between the priory and the townspeople. These were at least partly resolved in 1300 when an agreement was reached between the Prior of Lenton and the Mayor of Nottingham. This reduced the fair to eight days again and allowed Nottingham merchants to hire booths at the fair, though only for the sale of their own wares.

The fair came to resemble a small town, made up of booths which were thatched or tented, some with sleeping quarters behind them. There is evidence of repairs to booths by carpenters costing 1s 3d for five days work. The stalls were laid out in rows selling specific goods, similar units being grouped together; virtually every type of commodity was represented. The fair was opened by the Mayor of Nottingham and became a great annual occasion. Ostensibly the fair was worth only about £35 a year to the priory, but it seems likely that the right the priory had of the first choice of goods from every stallholder was much more valuable. The priory also enjoyed the profits of a special court set up to deal with miscreants.

Monastic Life

Throughout its existence the life of the priory was disrupted by the strife arising from the collection of the Peak District tithes from William Peveril's original endowment. Peveril's estates were confiscated by Henry II, who gave three Peak District churches and their appurtenances to various parties, the rights eventually being transferred to the Dean and Chapter of Lichfield. This provoked Lenton to pursue litigation over its rights in the matter, which proved a major financial burden to the priory. Ultimately Lenton's monks resorted to acts of violence and a total disregard for the right of sanctuary. The most notable of these occasions was in 1250, when the monks forcibly seized tithes of wool and lambs from the church at Tideswell, Derbyshire, where they had been placed in the nave of the church for safekeeping. During this affray eighteen lambs were accidentally killed, and fourteen were taken to Lenton grange. Tithes of geese, hay and oats were also seized by similar violent methods on other occasions, giving rise to considerable scandal. As a punishment for these offences, the Prior of Lenton was ordered to pay a fine of 100 marks to the Sacrist of Lichfield, as well as voluntary compensation to the Chapter for damages incurred.

The violence appears to have been in abeyance in 1262, when the Visitation report tells us that the behaviour of the inhabitants of Lenton Priory was 'all that could be desired'. A report thirteen years later said that the 27 monks and four lay brethren appeared 'to be behaving as directed'. But the following year the prior was involved in a case of fraud and robbery which culminated in him witnessing the murder of the rector's proctor in St George's churchyard, Barton-in-Fabis. The prior was later called to appear before Pope Urban IV, but he failed to do so and was subsequently excommunicated by the cardinal who was in charge of the affair. A less important concern arose several years later, when the monks' habits were reported to be red or russet in colour and a direction was made for them to be immediately replaced with a darker material 'as near black as possible'. The monks were once more leading 'good and commendable lives' when in 1279 the prior himself was appointed as Visitor of the Cluniac houses of England by the Abbot of Cluny. It is therefore assumed that the report's description of the Prior of Lenton as 'a worthy, good man of blameless repute' was written by the second appointed Visitor, the Prior of Mont-Didier.

Problems concerning the monks' behaviour arose again in the fourteenth century. In 1350 Prior Peter requested civil assistance to prevent three apostate monks of Lenton walking abroad in secular dress. During the latter part of the century the monks were reported to be in rebellious mood with outsiders supporting them against the prior with vandalism and theft resulting. Richard II requested the Archbishop of York to enquire into the dissentions, to correct defects and remove disobedient monks. But not all court cases involving Lenton Priory portrayed the monks as perpetrators of misdemeanour. The Nottingham borough court record of 1355 reports a case in which Walter the

Goldsmith used substandard materials for the repair of a crystal vessel, despite the fact that the prior had provided sufficient pure gold and silver.

In spite of these troubles, Lenton's priors were prominent in royal and ecclesiastical circles and much involved in the affairs of state. One prior, in particular, had an impact well outside the confines of the priory wall. Robert de Lexington was the middle of three brothers, each of whom attained high office in the reigns of John and Henry III, the eldest becoming Lord Keeper and the youngest, Bishop of Lincoln. Prior of Lenton for several years around 1220, Robert was primarily a royal servant and judge. In 1208-9 he was *custos* (custodian) of the Archbishopric of York during its vacancy. He became Prior of Lenton probably in 1215, but four years later was appointed a King's Justice Itinerant. His royal duties took over from his religious ones, for he was no longer prior in 1223 when Henry III put him in charge of the royal castles of the Peak and Bolsover. Robert was later made Governor of Oxford castle. He continued as a judge until 1243, by which time he had long been the oldest legal officer in the kingdom. Though 'struck by palsy' he lived on, according to Matthew Paris, until 1250, 'having acquired a distinguished name and ample possessions'.

The thirteenth century was a particularly busy period of building, business and entertainment, with many records of the priors' travels abroad. The King also called upon the prior to attend at Blyth on several occasions to prohibit the tournament. His presence was required as moral backing for the royal order of prohibition on activities considered likely to escalate into riotous behaviour. Royal documents also record the entertainment of kings, archbishops, bishops and members of the aristocracy on several occasions at Lenton, mainly in the thirteenth and fourteenth centuries. The comfort and food provided by the priory were often preferred to the facilities offered at Nottingham Castle. By contrast Lenton's almsgiving to the poor was comparatively small but included an anniversary distribution of £2 13s 4d in honour of William Peveril and his wife.

Thomas Elmham, appointed in 1414, was probably the most influential of the Lenton priors in national affairs, both as a royal chaplain to Henry V and as Vicar General to the Abbot of Cluny for England and Scotland. He attended the king at the battle of Agincourt and drafted documents for the Cluniac order, managing to fulfil all his duties to both masters for twelve years. He resigned as prior in 1426 when promoted to Commissary General for all vacant benefices belonging to the Cluniac order throughout the British Isles. He was the author of several works, including two on Henry V - a prose *Life* and *Versus Rythmici de Henrico Quinto*, which seem to have been written when he was a member of the royal household. In *Versus* he gives a detailed physical description of the King: 'His complexion is florid, his eyes bright, large and of an auburn tinge, dovelike when unmoved, and fierce as a lion when in anger'. His writings were characterised by a verbose style and vigorous attacks on the Lollards, whose views he described as 'everything most vile, most murderous and most sacrilegious'.[1]

After 1392 the procedure for appointing a new prior was changed. Sometimes he was appointed by the Prior of Lewes, the major Cluniac house in England. Then on an unprecedented occasion in 1459, the King granted the position to Thomas Wollore for life, disregarding the Abbot of Cluny and his Vicar General. But the Pope required Wollore's resignation on the grounds of his illegitimate birth and lack of the necessary dispensation. The Prior of Newstead then reinstated Wollore in accordance with the King's instructions. This incident successfully deprived the Abbot of Cluny of his previous right, after which he is said to have lost interest in the English province.

The priory exercised direct control over several parish churches including Beeston, the rectory of which was appropriated by Lenton in 1330 when the church became a chapel subject to Lenton Priory. The advowson of Nuthall church was also in the possession of Lenton as confirmed by Roger, Archbishop of York. Portions of stained glass removed from the priory church during the suppression are believed to have been taken to Nuthall for safe keeping and now probably form part of a window on the south side of the church.

Lenton had two dependent religious cells, one located within a cave near Nottingham Castle being known as St

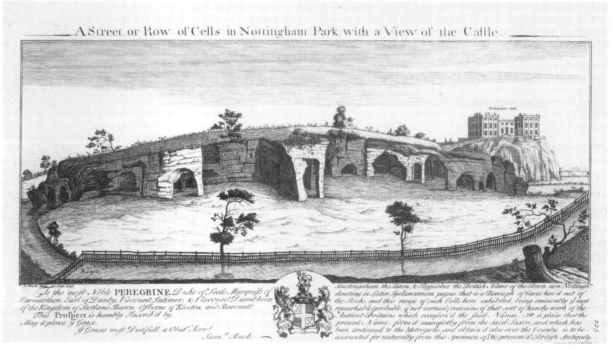

Samuel Buck's engraving , showing Lenton Priory's monastic cell, St Mary of the Rocks, 1726.

Mary le Roche (St Mary of the Rocks). It was apparently an idyllic spot where two monks were protected from the general populace by the intervening course of the river Leen but were able to observe courtiers and royal guests crossing the meadows. Here the monks tended a garden and kept a boat upon the river. They were allowed 4d per day for celebrating daily divine services for the souls of the King's ancestors.

The Dissolution

The names of several priors in the late Middle Ages, such as John Ilkeston and Thomas Nottingham, indicate that local men were influential in its affairs. In 1534 Sir Anthony Babington asked Thomas Cromwell to choose a successor to John Annesley from the monks at Lenton, stating that this would be preferable to the introduction of a stranger. The prior appointed was the ill-fated Nicholas Heath, who was to become the victim of increasing political intrigue. Throughout his ensuing ordeal, Heath was supported by Sir John Willoughby of Wollaton, who was an ardent believer in the 'old religion'. He was uneasy about the campaign of accusation against Heath and supported his complaint about the behaviour of a monk called Hamlet Pentriche, who had fled from the priory several times, in the last instance taking monastic goods and depositing them in the hands of his abettors in Nottingham. Sir John's support was not entirely selfless; he had a vested interest in co-operation with the monks, as the draining sough for his Wollaton coal pits ran across the priory land down to the river. Outside pressures increased upon Lenton, until finally their internal unity was tested to the ultimate.

At the time of the Dissolution there is evidence that Lenton antagonised Cromwell with its debts and associated problems, especially when monastic plate was sold to a London goldsmith in an effort to improve the finances of the house. Nicholas Heath also appears to have fallen foul of extortion by Cromwell. In a letter to him written in June 1536, Heath asks that Cromwell will accept £60 and remit the remaining £40 owed until Martinmas, this payment being connected with his promotion to Lenton 'through your favour'. There is an obvious implication of simony; a payment requested for the bestowing of the position of prior upon Heath.

A large fee paid for denization had increased the priory's debt, but the *Valor Ecclesiasticus* shows a net annual income of £336. For this reason it could not be placed amongst the smaller houses and might be considered 'rich pickings' for a bankrupt monarchy. These factors combined to encourage Cromwell to be rid of Lenton whose possessions would be of distinct financial advantage to the Crown. If surrender was not to be effected, then other means of closure were to be manipulated by the exploitation of disunity, so erasing Cromwell's annoyance and satisfying the avarice of Henry VIII.

Documents amongst the *Letters and Papers of Henry VIII* show Hamlet Pentriche to be the key figure in the ensuing drama. In a letter to Cromwell, for example, he requests that he be allowed to give evidence of slanderous words spoken by the monks against the King and Queen and against Cromwell. The evidence presented was of a conversation between a group of monks who were criticising the activities of the government at about the time of the Pilgrimage of Grace. The conversation is said to have taken place whilst they were sitting near the fire in the misericorde at Lenton. Cromwell was mentioned and was described by Pentriche as one ' whom they love worst of any man in the world'. Pentriche states that the prior and his council spent the week following this incident fabricating a case against him, and asks that any counter accusations that they might make be treated with caution as he was now fearful for his life. Once more, Sir John Willoughby attempted to defend Lenton, asking that Pentriche be punished for falsehood; he was unsuccessful. Pentriche was at this time languishing in the Fleet prison.

The accusation carried considerable weight against the house, and the cohesion of its monks fell into disarray. Thomas Cromwell had now been handed ideal evidence for use under the new Verbal Treason Act, and in February 1538 Nicholas Heath was thrown into prison. Several of the gentry and Nottingham merchants, who were probably swept along on the general tide of revulsion against the monks' indolent lifestyle, and thinking of their own possible gain, had little compunction in colluding in Heath's downfall.

Prior Heath along with one of his monks, probably Ralph

Swenson, was eventually convicted of treason and hanged, drawn and quartered two miles away in Nottingham in March 1538 and their mutilated remains displayed at the gate of the priory. There is a record of wine bought for the judges on the fateful day and expenses paid for cleaning Cow Lane (Clumber Street) which was the traditional approach to the place of execution in the market square. Had the monks of Lenton voluntarily surrendered, closure would have resulted in the community being pensioned off and none of these bloody and dramatic events taking place. In the event, the priory was suppressed by attainder and the monks were cast out without any means of support. The humiliation dealt to the house was intended to serve as an example to other houses which had not yet succumbed to pressure from the Crown.

Later History

The circumstances of the executions at Lenton meant that the revenues and raw materials from the priory went automatically to the King. Sir John Willoughby, as steward of the former priory, was conveniently situated to benefit by acquiring the property, but failed to do so. His interest lay mainly in the religious heritage. The medieval service books were saved by him perhaps in hope of their re-use, and at a later date he is known to have had at least one ex-Lenton monk as a tutor within his household.

In 1539 Henry VIII granted the site of Lenton Priory and its demesne to Sir Michael Stanhope on a 40-year lease; but Stanhope became involved in political intrigue and was executed in 1552. A rental document of 1554 gives a description of the conventual buildings at that time. The 'great church' is mentioned only as 'a source of free stone', but three other buildings within the precinct are described. There was 'the mansion', containing two parlours on the ground floor and two chambers on the first floor, with various other rooms adjoining. This probably constituted the east range of the cloisters. There is also mention of 'houses of office' (said to mean the reredorter), as well as 'fair great lodging of brick and timber' presumed to have been the prior's lodgings. It was possibly built at the same time as the brick tower at Aspley Hall, Nottingham, the original building at Aspley being the prior's hunting lodge. Also listed are the inner gate house with three rooms above,

described as in a 'decayed state'; the outer gate house with hall above and inner rooms, 'where courts were held'; also the fair booths. Farm and outbuildings complete the listing of those structures which had survived the sixteen years since the Dissolution.

A letter of 1555 confirmed that the 198 fodders of lead previously received in London for the King's use were from Lenton. Excavation evidence suggests that the roof was fired at some stage, although it is thought that the buildings eventually collapsed due to weathering after the removal of the lead from the roof. Assizes were held in 1573 at Lenton Priory, however, confirming that the buildings were not at that time wholly destroyed. Later material was taken from the site for use in the building of Wollaton Hall, which was completed in 1588. Several pieces of carved stone have recently been identified within the wall foundation of the steward's room and provenanced to Lenton. Despite continued removal of stone, part of the church was still standing in 1601 when the baptism of Thomas Bradford was recorded there. The last remaining part of the church disappeared when the steeple fell and the stone was used for a local causeway in 1677.

In 1604 Sir Michael Hicks purchased the demesne land and a rental agreement with Sir Percy Willoughby mentions a cottage called 'Brickhouse' which continues throughout the records up to 1630. This can be assumed to be the remains of the brick-built 'prior's lodging' previously mentioned. Seventeenth and eighteenth century owners of the priory demesne lands tended to be absentee landlords interested only in rent returns for grazing and pasture, but in 1798 the area now constituting the main campus of the University of Nottingham was bought for £36,000 by Thomas Pares and Thomas Paget, gentleman bankers of Leicester. Almost immediately, most was portioned off and resold at considerable profit. Prestigious family houses were built, many of which still stand as part of the University heritage.

The priory site was bought in 1802 by William Stretton. He subsequently built the house called Lenton Priory for his own occupation. Stretton was an accomplished architect, builder and antiquarian; but his principal interest was in archaeological artefacts rather than in creating a site plan. Many interesting finds are recorded in his manuscripts, and

Detail from a map of Sherwood Forest c.1500, showing Lenton Priory, contemporarily described as 'Lenton Habay'

the tiles and other objects found are now in Nottingham Museums collections. After William Stretton's death in 1828, 'The Priory' was intermittently occupied by his family and let to industrialists, and at the beginning of the 1880s the Sisters of Nazareth took up residence, restoring part of the site to its original use as a religious house.

From 1884 onwards the area around the original priory became over-built by expanding industrial buildings and workers' housing, some of which covered the conventual church site. The probable site of some medieval workshops hosted a large factory and a public house. In the twentieth century Nazareth House extended further over the monastic cloister area and the 'Priory Church of St Anthony' was built on the foundations of the monastic infirmary chapel. In the 1960s the demolition of three houses on Priory Street enabled further excavations, while a major engineering project canalised the flow of the river Leen in a direct course to the river Trent.

There are many fragmentary remains of Lenton Priory bearing witness to its days of greatness. One of the most important is the *pulpitum* altar stone excavated in the 1960s. It now forms the base of the high altar in St Lawrence's church, Long Eaton. Priory life is also recalled by the wax impressions of six seals, two attached to

documents at Lichfield, the others being at King's College, Cambridge. But the most striking artefacts must be the Norman font and a large corbel head. The latter was authenticated by Professor Maurice Barley as a piece of fifteenth century carving from Lenton; it possibly represented a monarch or a religious personage, the weathered shaping on the head suggesting a crown or mitre. It is in private hands. Finest of all, the magnificent font of the conventual church, demonstrating superlative early Norman workmanship, can be viewed within Holy Trinity church, Lenton.

References

1. J.T. Godfrey, *The History of the Parish and Priory of Lenton* (London and Derby, 1884), 184, 186

Access

OS SK 552 387. Site north of Dunkirk Flyover (A52), reached via Abbey Street (A453). Visible remains *in situ* including a pillar base, the north wall foundation and the north western corner of the transept. These can be seen from Priory Street, Old Church Street and St Antony's church graveyard.

Thurgarton Priory

John Hamilton and Sue Terry

T hurgarton in the early twelfth century was a place of ancient settlement and local significance. It lay beside a small stream in fertile farmland on the edge of the Trent floodplain some ten miles north-east of Nottingham and close to an important crossing of the river which connected to the nearby Fosse Way. The area had been farmed in Roman times and, judging by the name, came under the control of a Danish lord sometime before the Conquest, giving its name to the local wapentake. At Domesday it had a church and was noted as one of the 34 Nottinghamshire manors granted to Walter 1st Baron Deyncourt by William I.

Walter's son Ralph was persuaded by Archbishop Thurstan of York to found a house of Augustinian canons. When Thurstan took over the archbishopric in 1119, there was a notable lack of religious houses in Nottinghamshire, with only Blyth and the recently established Lenton. But there was also a lack of locally-based magnates of the first order with the resources to found the traditional Benedictine or Cluniac houses. The Deyncourt estates were in fact centred on the Kesteven area of Lincolnshire not far across the Trent, but they were not of the first rank. An Augustinian house, however, was comparatively cheap to establish, requiring only a limited endowment of land and some churches which the canons would serve.

Because of its position and local importance, Thurgarton was perhaps an obvious place to choose for the new priory in spite of being only a few miles from the major collegiate church at Southwell. In addition, as the earliest charter states, some canons were already attached to the church and thus able to form the basis of the new house (a not unusual procedure for Augustinian foundations). This charter, drawn up by Thurstan probably around 1130, states

that Ralph granted to St Peter's Thurgarton and to the regular canons 'of the same place' three churches, a mill and 40 bovates of land. This perhaps made little change to the existing establishment beyond adding to its wealth. Ralph's own charter, which can almost certainly be dated between 1140 and 1145, was drawn up after Thurstan's death and mentions the foundation of a house of religion for the first time. Moreover, it was placed first in the Thurgarton Cartulary, indicating its central importance in the eyes of the priory's authorities.

The canons were perhaps in temporary residence at Fiskerton for some time just before this, suggesting the lack of suitable accommodation at Thurgarton. The substantive life of the new priory, therefore, seems to begin with this second charter. Ralph now added substantially to his original endowment. The priory was given all of the manors of Thurgarton and Fiskerton, together with the dues from eleven churches. Ironically, having apparently spent some effort founding the priory, Ralph Deyncourt and his heirs seem to have taken little further interest in it. It was by no means unusual for founding families to continue to add endowments, but with minor exceptions the Deyncourts did not do this. Instead Walter, the third baron, lavished his benefactions on Kirkstead Abbey in Lincolnshire.

One of the oak misericords showing a robed figure

The Deyncourt grants had left Thurgarton reasonably endowed, and it could have lived on these. It owed its rise as the second largest house in Nottinghamshire to the energetic canvassing of further grants by the early priors. They were successful in gaining the interest of several other families, of whom the de Vilers were among the first and most important. Matthew de Vilers and his brother Roger, who became a canon at Thurgarton, granted land in the nearby Bingham wapentake. With new benefactors like these and using spare funds to purchase more land, the priory was able to increase its holdings throughout the thirteenth and into the fourteenth century, by which time it had property in 74 vills mostly in conveniently consolidated holdings. Fifty six of these vills were in Nottinghamshire, and the rest in Lincolnshire and Derbyshire, including the towns of Nottingham, Lincoln and Boston.

Architectural History

There was a church at Thurgarton at the time of Domesday. By 1120, as mentioned, this was already the base for some regular canons, but its siting and construction are unknown. The small chapel, found on Castle Hill next to the priory and probably dating from the first half of the twelfth century, was perhaps a dependent chapel, succeeded on the same site by a mortuary chapel serving the priory. The positioning of the priory close to the village (quite different from nearby Shelford) suggests it used the site of the parish church. The apparent temporary residence of the canons at nearby Fiskerton for some years after the foundation supports this.

Building for the new priory probably began soon after the original foundation. But nothing of the first building survives, it being replaced early in the next century. Since the priory church or part of it was also the parish church, the western part survived the Dissolution largely intact. The remains - the columns supporting three bays of the nave, the fine north-west tower with its lancet windows and moulding, and the west doorway with its beautiful dog toothed decoration - are all in the Early English style of the first half of the thirteenth century. Moreover, the Close Rolls of 1228 and 1236 record grants of 23 oaks from Sherwood Forest for the fabric of the church. The full size and precise construction of the church are unknown, but the remains indicate a second tower at the west end and a roof much higher than that of the present parish church, allowing a triforium and clerestory windows. This evidence and Thurgarton's wealth suggest it may well have rivalled Southwell Minster.

Three oak misericord stalls showing left to right, a robed figure, a bearded head and foliage. Angelic figures stand beside the uprights

Work on the other priory buildings was also in progress during the thirteenth century. A further sixteen oaks were given by the King in the 1250s for construction works, presumably for these other buildings, since there is no mention of the church in the record. In the cellar of the present house alongside the church there survive five double bays formed of squat piers with almost rounded arches surmounted by quadripartite vaulting, typical of this period. These comprised the ground floor of the west side of the cloister and probably served as a *cellarium*. Later in the century the church seems to have been altered or extended; just before the remodelling of the parish church in the 1850s, a visitor noted 'a peculiarly rich and delicately

might be expedient for the sleeping of the canons, though whether this meant additional accommodation or the renovation of existing cells, is not certain.

Beyond this, we have no certain information on the priory buildings. But up to the late eighteenth century there was a magnificent kitchen to the south of the surviving *cellarium* and this is shown on Buck's print of 1726. At its demolition in 1777 it was believed to be a survival from the priory and there seems no good reason for it to have been built subsequently. It was described as 'vast and magnificent, almost beyond parallel or comparison ... (a) noble monument of ancient grandeur'.[1] Surviving stonework

The West Profpect of Thurgarton Priory, near Newark, in the County of Nottingham.

Samuel Buck's engraving of the west prospect of Thurgarton Priory, 1726

moulded double window ... of a very beautiful Early Decorated style' which must have been moved from the original church. A set of three oak misericord stalls of the same period and a statue niche with canopy in the late Decorated style also survive. Little is known of the later history of the priory buildings. In 1402 Pope Boniface IX approved the renewal of as many cells in the dormitory as

indicates it straddled the stream. Downstream, more prosaically, further stonework hints at the site of the reredorter. At its height, then, Thurgarton priory was a substantial monastic establishment, comprising a major conventual church with a cloister to the south surrounded by priory buildings, which extended to the specially diverted stream.

Economic History

As already noted, the priory was well supported financially from the start. Not only was Ralph Deyncourt's endowment generous, but the priory in Nottinghamshire was successful in obtaining further gifts. By 1291 its taxable income was £248, second only to Lenton Priory. This income was split one-third spiritualities and two-thirds temporalities. The proportion of temporalities was unusually high and apparently the result of deliberate policy. Unlike Lenton, whose numerous properties were widely scattered and more heavily dependent on tithes, Thurgarton was careful to acquire agricultural holdings in consolidated groups, particularly in the first half of the fourteenth century. The priory grouped its local properties into seven demesne 'manors' based only a few miles from Thurgarton on either side of the Trent. These provided income in the form of both rents and produce and were more efficient to administer than the collection of tithes from far-flung places.

These manors formed the backbone of the priory's estate; a survey of 1328 valued the priory's income at nearly £240. Thurgarton itself produced £85, including profits from the court, four mills and the villagers' rent and services, and Fiskerton £30. The impression that the estate was well run at this time is reinforced by the detailed nature of the survey. It states, for example, that each villager must provide a cock and a hen annually besides a rent of 4-5s for a villein or 2-3s for a cottager. They also had to perform agricultural services for the priory using their own ploughs and carts, and provide carriage with a horse three times a year from the priory's 'foreign' (i.e. outside the village) granges.

In return the priory had to do little more than provide a meal on the second day of Christmas, and bread when labour was given - plus two herrings to harrowers. There is no sign that the canons conceived that being improving landlords was part of their duty. The survey also throws light on contemporary attitudes to sex; each 'she villein' had to pay 5s 4d for the redemption of her soul when she married or committed fornication. Inside or outside marriage sex was considered impure for women.

Although the villeins' labour was valued at 13s 4d, the round figure suggests this was for taxation purposes only. There is no indication that labour services were being commuted for monetary payments at this time. Moreover, the charter's concentration on arable activities, the four mills and the lack of mention of either sheep or cattle all imply that crop husbandry was the major agricultural activity at Thurgarton. Otherwise there is little information on the priory's economic activities. It had pasture for 160 sheep in Derbyshire, and its holding in Boston, an important port, may imply involvement in trade.

The years of good management were followed by decades of trouble. From 1276 to 1304, successive Archbishops of York were concerned about Thurgarton's affairs. Much of this centred on the election of successive priors as well as their and the canons' behaviour; but administration also caused the authorities much anxiety. For example, in 1276 Archbishop Giffard demanded that the church's leaking roof and the priory's outer perimeter be repaired. Basically the problem seems to have been caused by incompetent management and lack of a centralised accounting system, rather than real financial trouble at this time.

That arose early in the fifteenth century. In 1401 Boniface IX issued an indulgence to penitents who gave alms for the conservation of the priory, which suggests it was in need of funds for repairs. In 1415 Thurgarton priory (with several others) was relieved of half its tax assessment 'because of excessive assessments and insupportable losses'. Six years later the priory again had its tax assessment halved 'on account of the threatened collapse of the church'. The continuing outbreaks of the Black Death had doubtless produced a major shortfall in the priory's income.

In 1534 the priory's income was £361 gross, showing a healthy increase over 1291 and still second only to Lenton. Temporalities had become less dominant as a source of income and were close to the average for Nottinghamshire monasteries at this valuation. Deductions, however, amounted to £101 and included £44 for chantries. Nevertheless, the probability is that the priory had sufficient funds up to the Dissolution to prosper, if competently and honestly managed.

Monastic Life

The history of Thurgarton priory provides good examples of both the sanctity that was attained and the scandal that could arise in Nottinghamshire monasteries. Though one of the richest houses in the county, the priory probably never held more than twenty or so canons. From this number Augustinian canons had to be found to serve local parish churches such as Fiskerton and Lowdham. Such names as we have of these men - Walter de Bingham, Robert de Basford and Alexander de Gedling - suggest that they were mainly recruited locally. Nevertheless, Thurgarton was important regionally if not nationally. It was one of the few priories (out of 274 Augustinian houses in England) where the annual chapter of the Order was held. Moreover, in the 1340s the prior with his colleague at Shelford was involved in the delicate task of assessing and levying taxes for Edward III.

From 1276 the priory suffered 40 years of scandal, discord and mismanagement. In that year Archbishop Giffard found it necessary to issue injunctions to the prior and canons on many matters but especially monetary control and vagrancy. These were continuing themes, to which were added the problems of disruptive canons, disputed elections and sexual impropriety. Giffard's injunctions against canons who went out of the monastery to enjoy the company of friends moved Brother Hugh de Farndon to write a pamphlet attacking the Archbishop, the prior and other canons. This and his generally disruptive behaviour led to his imprisonment.

But more serious trouble arose in the 1280s. Two disputed elections for prior in 1284 had to be quashed for irregularities before Archbishop Wickwane appointed Gilbert de Ponteburgh (Boroughbridge) from Nostell priory, with which Thurgarton had reciprocal arrangements. Within two years Gilbert had to purge himself of alleged adultery with a local married woman. A few months later Alexander de Gedling was reproved for bad language during a meeting of the chapter, and worse, in 1290 Walter de Bingham was excommunicated for assaulting John de Sutton in church. Gilbert resigned as prior, wishing to return to Nostell, and Alexander de Gedling was installed in his place. This produced even deeper trouble.

In 1295 Richard Maluvel, who had earlier sought permission to enter a stricter order, wandered around pretending to find a house to accept him. Hugh de Farndon was also found that year vagrant and destitute, as he was again in 1302. Walter de Bingham too was vagrant in 1301, yet astonishingly he was appointed Prior of St Oswald's, Gloucester, a post he held for several years before being removed, reinstated and removed again, all in the space of two years, before finally returning to Thurgarton in 1312. Here he was in trouble three years later for failing to say Mass; his punishment included a diet of bread, beer and vegetables for seven Fridays and the reciting of seven psalters in seven weeks.

At the beginning of the fourteenth century the priory was in financial difficulty. Alexander seems to have got the priory into debt by alienating property, causing loss of income. This led to lawsuits by creditors, who included the Sheriff of Nottingham on behalf of the Crown, to recover their debts; these actions in turn involved the priory in further expenditure. The visit of Edward I in April 1303 in the midst of this produced only a grant of a pension out of the priory's funds. Archbishop Corbridge then deposed Prior Alexander. But the canons, though at first split on the issue, requested his reinstatement since his deposition had only worsened the situation, causing creditors to press harder for payment and making the recovery of their rights to certain properties impossibly expensive. Their plight, they claimed, was due more to the cost of lawsuits than extravagance or mismanagement. At first Corbridge refused to accept that the situation demanded Alexander's reinstatement, but after quashing two elections he accepted his candidacy.

After a few quieter years trouble arose again in 1315 when Prior John de Rudestan was 'incontinent' (that is, had sexual relations) with Alice Cade of Thurgarton, as was Brother Henry of Norwell with another woman. The next year John was deposed apparently following fraud by him and some of the canons. Thereafter the priory seems to have become better run both spiritually and financially. No doubt the attempt by the authorities to impose central accountancy procedures on Augustinian houses from 1220 onwards met resentment and reluctance to change. But in Thurgarton's case the evidence points to a lack of suitable candidates for the office of prior. As elsewhere, for example at Newstead, it seems likely the position of prior in *loco Dei* went to the head of some of those appointed, faced, as they suddenly were, with almost unchecked powers of management and access to considerable sums of money.

Painting on a nave pillar to commemorate the 600th anniversary of Walter Hilton's death

The life and works of Walter Hilton come as a salutary corrective to the picture of incompetence and self-indulgence painted by the history of the period just described. In fact, little is known of his early life. It is likely he was born in the 1330s and studied law at Cambridge. He tried the life of a hermit, but abandoned it and came to Thurgarton sometime after 1375. Why he chose Thurgarton is not known, but at the very least it suggests the priory's troubles were long since over. Over the next twenty years, until his death in 1396, he wrote and corresponded widely, establishing himself as one of the group of outstanding English 'mystics' who flourished at this time, including Richard Rolle and Julian of Norwich.

Through his writings Hilton emerges as a warm and gentle personality, full of humility, yet down to earth and eager to help those who sought his advice. Indeed, he seems to have established a reputation as a spiritual adviser and the first part of his most famous work, *The Ladder* (or *Scale*) *of Perfection,* is addressed to an individual anchoress. But he was conscious, too, of a wider potential audience, and the second part, which was produced quite separately some ten years later shortly before his death, is written more generally. He has no claim to be an innovative theologian; his importance lies in his ability to translate the religious insights of others into practical guidance for those truly seeking progress in their spiritual journey.

It was a commonplace of his time to contrast the contemplative life of the monks in their cloister with the active life of both clerics and lay people 'in the community', as we would now say. Hilton accepted current belief that the former was closer to God, but urged the 'active' to make prayer and contemplation part of their life. He taught there were three levels of religious life: the unreformed state; reformation in faith but not in feeling; and finally reformation in both faith and feeling. He encouraged all to move higher up the scale of religious life particularly towards reformation in feeling.

Hilton is also important because he wrote in English at a crucial time in the development of the language (he was an almost exact contemporary of Chaucer); and although his prose style was not especially noteworthy, he helped to establish English as an effective medium for literature of all kinds. His writings quickly became popular and widely read, as the large number of extant manuscripts shows. They were translated into Latin and printed as early as 1494. Sir Thomas More recommended *The Ladder* to his gaoler in the Tower. His humble, clear and methodical teachings struck a chord in the minds of many in the years up to the Reformation and beyond. Ironically, though his work is clearly based on the presumption of Catholic faith, his encouragement of laymen to seek a closer union with God for themselves, may have helped to create a body of educated and devout Christians, who found much to criticise in the less holy activities of Hilton's Church.

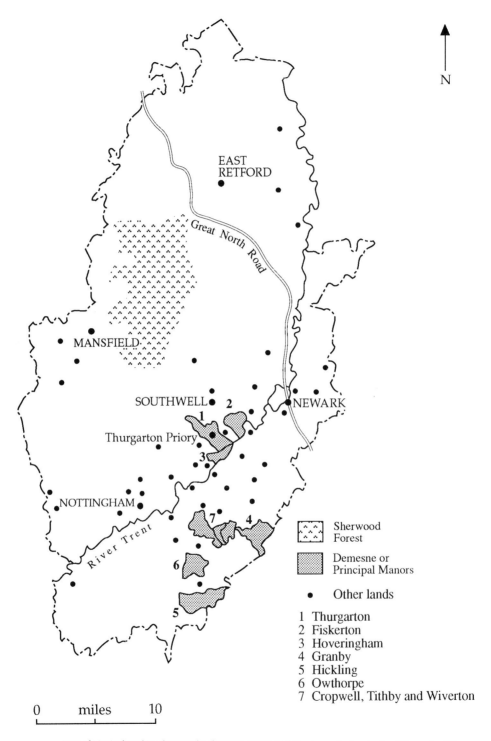

N

EAST
RETFORD

Great North Road

MANSFIELD

Sherwood
Forest

Demesne or
Principal Manors

•   Other lands

SOUTHWELL   2

1

Thurgarton Priory

3

NEWARK

NOTTINGHAM

River Trent

7

4

6

5

1 Thurgarton
2 Fiskerton
3 Hoveringham
4 Granby
5 Hickling
6 Owthorpe
7 Cropwell, Tithby and Wiverton

0   miles   10

Map of Nottinghamshire showing the demesne or principal manors and other lands of Thurgarton Priory

The Dissolution

The priory was visited by Layton and Legh in 1536, when 'they surpassed themselves in the wholesale character of their hideous charges' against the inmates. According to their report 'ten (canons) were guilty of unnatural offences, that the prior had been incontinent with several women, that six others with both married and single women (and) that eight of the canons desired to be released from their vows'.[2] Eight canons later signed the surrender document, the same number as the report claims desired release. This suggests that the charges of sexual misbehaviour involving sixteen canons plus the prior were either exaggerated, invented or refer to the whole history of the priory. The generosity of the pensions granted to the prior, in particular, throw further doubt on the trustworthiness of the report.

Whatever the reliability of the charges, on 14 June 1538 Prior John Berwick signed the surrender document for Dr Legh. It was also signed and witnessed by William Chace, sub-prior, and John Champney, John Langeskar, John Ryley, Richard Leke, Robert Cant, Henry Gaskin and Richard Hopkyn, canons. John Berwick was granted Fiskerton Hall with chapel, gardens, stable, two meadows, tithes of hay and £40 *per annum* - a generous settlement which no doubt facilitated a most comfortable retirement. The sub-prior was the recipient of the next highest pension of £6 13s 4d *per annum*. The other canons each received £5 a year. The normal practice was for the pensions to be paid annually unless the recipient obtained alternative employment, at which time the pension ceased. But five former canons were still receiving these pensions in 1556.

Later History

After a few years in royal hands, Henry VIII granted the priory's lands in and around Thurgarton as well as the advowson of the church, to his newly founded Trinity College, Cambridge. The college continued to hold most of this land down the centuries, and still in 1922 was cited as the largest landowner in the village. Probably most of the conventual church was quickly pulled down, but part was retained as the parish church. In 1797 this was described as consisting of one dark aisle. Indeed, over the years Thurgarton parishioners seem to have been poorly served; in the eighteenth century the sacrament was administered only three times a year. It was not until 1852-4 that major restoration work was put in hand by the then owner of the priory, Richard Millward, who employed the well-known Nottingham architect T.C. Hine to produce the church as it stands today.

The rest of the priory buildings were bought from the Crown by William Cooper for £510 in 1539. Cooper, in the king's service in London, also leased land locally from Trinity College and became, in effect, lord of the manor. He quickly converted the west side of the cloister into a substantial residence. Further work on the house was done at the end of the century, but the property was much damaged by Parliamentary troops during the Civil War, for the Coopers were very active on the Royalist side. Later a Gilbert cousin took over the property and in 1777 John Gilbert Cooper demolished the surviving remains of the original buildings above ground, including the magnificent kitchen. This Cooper, a would-be arbiter of taste dubbed the Punchinello of Literature by Dr Johnson, built the present house. For twenty years from 1884 it was the first bishops' palace of the new diocese of Nottingham, but since then has been used mostly for commercial purposes.

References

1. R. Dickinson, *The History and Antiquities of the Town of Southwell* 3rd ed. (London, 1819, reprinted 1996), 303

2. W. Page (ed.), *Victoria County History of Nottinghamshire*, vol. II, 125

Access
OS 692492. What is left of the conventual church now forms part of Thurgarton parish church, which is approached up a lane running west off the main village street (A612). Unfortunately the magnificent west front of the church together with other priory remains are on private property.

Wallingwells Priory

Jane Johnson

allingwells nunnery was dedicated to St Mary and was situated near Carlton-in-Lindrick in north-west Nottinghamshire. It was an independent Benedictine priory founded some time between 1135 and 1154 by Ralph de Chevrecort during the reign of Stephen. Ralph's grant, dedicated 'to Almighty God and the Virgin St Mary', was of 'a place in his park at Carlton-by-the-Wells, to make and build there an inhabitation for holy religion, so free that its place shall not depend on or belong to any other place'. He called it Waldon-de-Wells from its situation among 'wells, fountains and streams', from which the modern name of Wallingwells is derived. Indeed, streams and waterways are still in evidence today. Ralph intended that his generosity should 'ensure the remission of his sin and for the good estate and the health of himself and his heirs and progeny and of all who should help and maintain the house'. His initial endowment included water for the mill, pasture in the parkland for beasts and pannage for swine, along with the right of way through his park when carting crops. The priory was granted rights of common pasture, lands and underwood, and the common rights in the field of Carlton.

The community lived frugally and piously; Archbishop Godfrey in 1262 described the nuns as being devout and poor. The nuns were assigned the corn tithes of eighteen bovates of land in Carlton free of all tithes great or small. Carlton rectory gave a pension of 20s and Cantley, Yorkshire, two marks in pension. In a later Visitation Archbishop Giffard gave his consent for the church at Cantley to be appropriated to the nuns on account of their penury and devout life. In 1291 its taxable income was less than £16. Later it was said that 'in the house were nine persons besides the prioress, all of good life and conversation, who desire to continue religious; the house well reputed, and good hospitality there daily kept. The moveable goods worth £52 3s 8¼d; no debts owing to the house.'[1] This description from the White Manuscripts is undated, but in 1536 when Layton and Legh visited it was valued at £60 *per annum*; more than a third of this was paid out in pensions, mostly to the vicar of Campsall, Yorkshire.

Layton and Legh could find no scandal but recorded as 'superstitious' the comb of St Edmund and an image of the Virgin said to have been discovered at the founding of the house. Wallingwells obtained a license exempting it from the effects of the 1536 Act and on 2 June 1537 the prioress, Margaret Goldsmith, entered into a covenant with Richard Oglethorp demising to him the whole monastery and all its possessions for the term of 21 years. The church at Wallingwells, the prioress's chambers, the dormitory, infirmary and other conventual buildings were reserved for the prioress and the convent. Oglethorp was entitled to cut down and carry away timber and underwood, but was to provide at his own cost an able priest to sing and read in the monastery, and pay yearly endowments to the nuns and their servants. He also had to provide commodities in the form of cattle and cereal crops, salt and oatmeal, coal, wood and candles as well as 40s for the nuns to enjoy fresh fish when they wished. Effectively he had become the financial manager of all their affairs.

But the new arrangement was not to last long. On 14 December 1539 the monastery was surrendered and pensions given to the prioress, sub-prioress and the remaining seven nuns. In 1562 the Crown sold the site to Sir Richard Pype. It subsequently passed through several hands before coming into the possession of the White family by marriage in 1698. Over the years the Whites built a substantial house, which they continued to own into the present century. In 1907 it was claimed that 'several of the original walls of the nunnery of great thickness remain'.[2]

Today nothing remains of Wallingwells except the foundations within the house, which has been converted into flats.

References

1. L. Jacks, *The Great Houses of Nottinghamshire and the County Families* (Nottingham, 1881), 151

2. M.H. Towry White, 'Some Account of the family of White of Tuxford and Wallingwells', *Transactions of the Thoroton Society* 11, 1907, 64

Access

OS SK573842. Today the area where Wallingwells nunnery stood is still woodland and open farmland, which can be explored by footpath and bridle paths from Carlton-in-Lindrick.

Broadholm Priory

David Crawford

Broadholm lay in a small projection of east Nottinghamshire in an area recently transferred to Lincolnshire. The hamlet, mentioned in Domesday, stands on a gravel terrace in low-lying swampy ground little more than twenty feet above sea-level between the rivers Trent and Witham. The area relies on deep ditches to allow the marshes to be used as good pasture and arable land. The site of the priory is a mile south of Fossdyke, a Roman drainage and navigational link between the two rivers and a busy trade route in the Middle Ages.

The priory was founded around 1145 for Premonstratensian canonesses by Agnes, wife of Peter de Golsa, who had himself just founded a Premonstratensian abbey at Newhouse, near Immingham, to which Broadholm was made subordinate. It was one of very few examples, nationally, of the Premonstratensian life adapted for nuns. It was poorly endowed from the start; Agnes's original grant was only worth £18 *per annum*. Gifts of land in and around Saxilby, a mile to the north, were added and possession confirmed by Sir Peter de Champagne, lord of the manor of Saxilby, who held the advowson of the priory and granted the convent free choice of prioress. Ralph de Albini, lord of the manor of South Ingleby, Lincolnshire a crusader who died at Acre in 1190, granted 'an orchard adjoining the churchyard of St Botolph's church in Saxilby (and) land between the sisters' courtyard and a grove of his, in free, pure, perpetual alms'. Other small gifts of land and buildings were added, mostly within four or five kilometres of Broadholm. In the thirteenth century the nuns were granted two quarters of corn (one wheat, one rye) which continued to be paid until the late nineteenth century from Grange Farm at Wigsley to the occupiers of Priory Farm at Broadholm. In 1201 Walter de Clifford and his wife gave St Helen's church at Thorney, together with 30 acres of land

and a mill on the moor. This became the mainstay of the convent, and in the *Taxatio* of 1291 the church at Thorney alone was worth £8 out of a total income of under £16. This would have been supplemented by the produce of the demesne lands.

Little has been discovered about the priory buildings at Broadholm. None remain standing and Manor Farm has been built using brick and blocks of stone, including parts of arches. Jurassic limestone at Lincoln Cliff would be the nearest source of building stone. From a comprehensive paper on Broadholm Priory published by the Rev R.E.G. Cole, rector of Doddington Pigot in 1905, we know that occasional finds have been made - bases of clustered columns, Early English arches and signs of dog-tooth ornament, the basin of a *piscina* - suggesting that the chapel was early thirteenth century. There are similarities to contemporary work at Lincoln Cathedral. The chapel stood behind the present farmhouse, while in a field to the east, skeletons showed the site of the cemetery. The large pool which Cole found in the field where the house stands has disappeared and cannot be located in aerial photographs taken between 1971 and 1984. There are crop-marks in surrounding fields but they require further research.

Broadholm was a small establishment with perhaps seven or eight nuns under a prioress; a reference in 1383 mentions the prioress's servants. The nunnery's affairs were supervised by the Abbot of Newhouse, 30 miles away, who appointed resident canons to act as chaplains, hear confessions and oversee the spiritual life of the nunnery. The prioress did not attend either the General or Provincial Chapters of the order held at Prémontré and Lincoln respectively.

Edward III's mother, Queen Isabella, was a loyal supporter of the prioress of Broadholm and helped settle disputes with the Abbot of Newhouse. In 1354 at the Queen's instigation a commission of four abbots met at Broadholm to mediate between the prioress, Joan de Reil, and Alan, the abbot. They decreed that: when a prioress was to be appointed, the abbot should investigate in chapter, under oath, the wishes of all the sisters and appoint as prioress the one favoured by them; all monies, the common seal and other treasures should be placed in a common chest with two locks, one key being held by the prioress and the other by a sister whom the rest should choose; to save expense only one canon from Newhouse should dwell with the sisters, to say mass for them daily and supervise their temporalities but not dispose of them against the will of the prioress; the father-abbot should four times a year hear or cause to be heard, without expense to them, the confessions of the prioress and sisters and should visit them for two days once a year with four or five carriages, and stay at their expense. The priory was not subject to archbishops' visitations, so one source of information on the sisters' lives is unavailable.

We may assume that during most of the 400 years of the nunnery's existence the tenor of life was peaceful since reported incidents are few and far between. Provided their tenants paid their rents, and grants of corn were forthcoming, the nuns could fulfil their lives of prayer and succour in the community and offer hospitality to visitors. But occasional upheavals occurred: in 1316 the right of the sisters of the order to go out from their cloisters was revoked 'because of a serious scandal'. What happened is not known and it may have arisen at Irford rather than Broadholm. More specific was an attack on 15 January 1350 when William Fox, the parson of Lea near Gainsborough, together with two friars from the Franciscan convent in Lincoln, violently took and carried away a nun, Margaret of Everingham, a sister at Broadholm, stripped her of her religious habit and clothed her in a green gown of secular fashion, taking also divers goods to the value of 40s. Margaret was probably the daughter of Sir Adam de Everingham of Laxton. The motive for this escapade is not known, nor the punishment. William Fox retained the rectory of Lea for 45 years.

Towards the end of the fourteenth century the villeins and common people were becoming more restless, questioning their servile status and demanding the disendowment of the church, and the free use of the forests. This may underlie another attack on the priory which induced the prioress to appeal to Richard II in 1383 for justice. She reported that William Wauterson and others had felled her trees and underwood, dug in her soil, carried off earth, trees and other goods, depastured her corn and grass, assaulted her servants and besieged her and her nuns in the priory and threatened them with death.

In 1505 the Abbot of Welbeck was appointed Commissary of the Abbot of Prémontré and undertook a Visitation to the houses of the order. He called at Broadholm, arriving there at the hour of dinner, and went on to spend the night in Lincoln at the expense of the Abbot of Tupholme. Doubtless he asked about the well-being of the community, but there is no record of his findings.

In 1534 papal jurisdiction over English monasteries was repudiated and the payment of annates and tenths was redirected to the English Crown. The *Valor Ecclesiasticus* recorded a net value for Broadholm of £16 5s 2d, so the Act of 1536 suppressing religious houses with an annual value of less than £200 sealed its fate. Dr London reported to Thomas Cromwell that he had taken the surrenders of several small nunneries at Kyme, Nun Cotham, Irford, Fosse ('a beggarly, poor and ruinous house'), Lincolnshire and Heynings, but there is no mention of Broadholm. It may already have been surrendered, since the last prioress, Joan Angevin, had been granted a pension of £4 13s 4d which she was still drawing in 1554. The fate of the remaining nuns is not known.

The King ordered the conventual buildings to be destroyed and the materials carried away. This would include the parts occupied by the nuns around the cloister, the chapel, the chapter house, refectory and dormitory. The prioress's lodging and farm may have been left for the benefit of a future tenant. In May 1537, the King granted a 21 year lease of the site and precincts of the priory, its windmill and demesne fields to Randolf Jackson, Chester Herald. The rent was £20 3s 8d per year, though the King retained the large trees for his own use. By about 1570 the property, which included dovecotes, gardens, orchards and a windmill, was sold by the Crown.

Access

OS SK 895 735. Manor Farm stands on the site of Broadholm Priory, 1 mile south of Saxilby. It is reached by a minor road turning off the road from Saxilby to Harby. Saxilby is 6 miles east-north-east from Lincoln on the A57(T) road to Worksop.

Rufford Abbey

Joy Bristow and Marie Wilkinson

Rufford, a medium-sized Cistercian house dedicated to St Mary the Virgin, was the fifth and last daughter house colonised from Rievaulx Abbey in Yorkshire. The first abbot was Gamellus and he came with twelve monks to found the abbey in 1146. The land had been bequeathed by Gilbert de Gaunt, Earl of Lincoln, when he was ill. He came from a very wealthy Anglo-Norman family who owned lands in the Midlands. Gilbert had been excommunicated by the Pope, and giving this land to found an abbey was by way of making amends for his previous behaviour.

In Stephen's reign Rufford was a desolate and wooded part of Sherwood Forest, some 24 miles north of Nottingham. The land itself was poor, and many of the charters endowing land mention the waste and assarting necessary to bring the land into cultivation. The abbey was built in a fertile area, adjacent to the villages of Rufford and Cratley and near to Rainworth Water, a small tributary of the river Maun. Eight families were living at Rufford when the monks came; but because the Order insisted the sites must be isolated, the villeins were persuaded to move, either by an exchange of land or being granted their freedom. By the end of the thirteenth century the village ceased to exist.

At Cratley, which had more fertile soil, the people were reluctant to go, and the monks spent many years bargaining with them. One William would only agree to release his land if the monks would give him right of burial, 30 marks and ten cows. He was given ten cows and ten marks in advance on condition he persuaded a certain Hugh to agree to exchange his lands, as Hugh's father had already agreed. Settlement was eventually reached and the abbot paid the remaining twenty marks. In another charter the landowner confirmed he would agree to his mother's grant of four

bovates in Cratley, if the monks would give him one mark and two measures of grain. Another instance shows the monks had to agree to give two carucates in Barton, 30 marks, 120 sheep and a palfrey in exchange. It took more than 100 years before the whole area was in the hands of the monks. Most of the displaced families went to better sites in Wellow or Edwinstowe.

After Gilbert's death disputes arose over his property, but in 1185 the monks obtained documents from Henry II confirming the earlier gifts. This stated that the abbey was under royal custody and protection. The 800-year-old document is one of the earliest surviving documents relating to Nottinghamshire. It was written in ink with a quill onto parchment which was made from a sheepskin. The ink could have been made from the galls of oak trees. The document has the impression of the Great Seal of England attached at the base of the document, and the reverse of the seal shows the king as an armed warrior on horseback.

Architectural History

Rufford Abbey was laid out in the usual Cistercian pattern, but with a slight difference. During building the church was extended, for the inner transept chapels are not in alignment with the aisles of the nave. This was discovered during excavations; perhaps the temporary church stood on the site and caused confusion during the laying of the piers and walls. From the walls still standing it is believed building was largely completed around 1170, and from these remains an idea of the size of the buildings can be gained. The discovery of the foundations of a large buttress at its south-east angle suggests that the south wall of the presbytery was rebuilt later in the Middle Ages. This would have caused some loss to the inner chapel of the south transept. Part of the lay brothers' quarters was incorporated in the house that was later built on the site, and the undercroft provides excellent examples of circular pillars and a groin-vaulted roof. Cupboards, perhaps for spoons and linens, can still be seen on the north wall and traces of the day stairs used by the community can be seen on the west wall.

The twelfth century gargoyle on the lay brothers' wall was one of the few decorations allowed by the Order. They

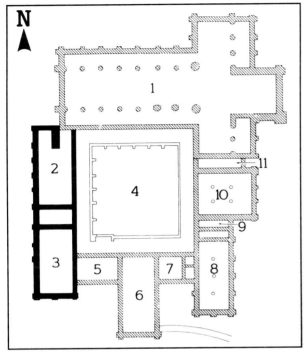

1. Church
2. Cellar
3. Lay brothers' frater
4. Cloister
5. Kitchen
6. Monks' frater
7. Warming house
8. Undercroft with dormitory over
9. Inner parlour
10. Chapter house
11. Sacristy
■ Surviving walls

were forbidden to have any stained glass windows, and no gold or jewels in their church plate. Their crucifixes were to be of painted wood. During early excavations a seven foot long slab was found, with the inscription in Latin stating it was over the tomb of Brother Robert de Markham, who died in April 1309 or 1329 (the date is indistinct). It is believed this came from the abbey church. The remains of many buildings, notably the gatehouse, the infirmary and the abbot's house still survive but are as yet unexcavated.

Economic History

Uniquely among Nottinghamshire religious houses, Rufford's original endowment apparently included no spiritualities. Nevertheless, Gilbert's original grants were sufficient to make it well up among the second rank of houses in wealth. Moreover, the abbey was successful in

adding to its endowment: over 1,000 charters still exist, describing gifts of land, rents and houses over the years. Donors often requested prayers to be said for them and their families in return. Much the most important acquisition was Rotherham in Yorkshire. By 1283 the abbey seems to have possessed a large part of the town as well as the rectory. Income arose from the court there as well as 'five mills under one roof', but mainly from rents and leases. So important was Rotherham to Rufford that by the Dissolution over half the abbey's 'free' taxable income came from the town.

The Cistercians, however, did not rely on such income. They were famous demesne farmers, making excellent use of their lay-brothers to work their land. The abbey organised much of its land holdings into 'granges'. Nine of these were established by 1218, and 21 in all. Most of these were in central Nottinghamshire within a few miles of Rufford. There were religious reasons for this; early statutes laid down that no grange was to be more than a day's journey away, so that the lay-brothers could return regularly for services. But it also made good economic sense, improving management control and reducing the time and expense spent on travelling. Four granges, however, were in Derbyshire, Barton being a full 55 miles from Rufford. But it seems to have played a key role in the abbey's valuable sheep farming activities, for it had pasture for 600 sheep, usable both for fattening lambs in summer and for overwintering. Nearer to home, Morton had pasture for 400 sheep, Boughton for 200 and Maplebeck for 100. Rufford, therefore, seems likely to have profited much from the wool trade.

The monks also held a weekly market and fair, and had the right to cut down and sell trees from the forest, large as well as the small ones called underwood. Some of this was used to make charcoal. In 1359 they received over £400 for wood. All this activity suggests that the abbey was in fact rather better off than the £177 of taxable income shown in the *Valor Ecclesiasticus* would indicate. Even that figure gave it above average wealth for Nottinghamshire monasteries.

Monastic Life

Little direct evidence of life at Rufford survives. As regards its religious aspects, the daily round of the dozen or so monks and their lay brothers was probably much the same as in Cistercian monasteries today, except that the services are now at slightly different times. The abbey was under the control of the mother house at Rievaulx and ultimately the founding house of the Order, the abbey of Citeaux. Visitations of Rufford were supposed to be made every two years. Little evidence for these survives, however, even of those of St Ailred, the much loved abbot of Rievaulx in the mid-twelfth century, whose book on Friendship is still widely read today.

One Visitation report to survive is that of the abbots of Loos and Tournay in France and Woburn, Bedfordshire, dated 26 May 1481.[1] The overall impression it gives is of a house that was running satisfactorily but not to the highest standards. Slackness and a failure to comply with the strict letter of the Rule were apparent in many aspects of daily life. 'At the name of Jesus and Mary let (the monks) always and everywhere bow their heads ... At the elevation of the Most Sacred Eucharist, when the bell sounds, let them bow their knees ... unless they are in the dormitory.' The rules of silence were not being strictly observed, 'we order that silence be kept in the four principal places - the church, the dormitory, the cloisters and the refectory'. Only when eating in the infirmary, where the religious should 'take their

The impressively vaulted lay brothers' refectory at Rufford Abbey

place separate from the seculars', could they speak to one another 'in a quiet manner' during meals, for the sake of recreation.

The music had been modernised without authorisation. The Visitors' very first injunction was that 'singing in the Divine Service ... should be done in a voice that is intelligible and in unison and without indulging in useless things'. It should be 'slower than at present' with good pauses in the middle of each verse. Clearly fancy part singing was to stop. The dress code, too, was to be rigorously enforced. Tunics were to be white, scapulas and sandals black. The habits must be 'made of cloth of serge or wool' and without trimmings. It seems, however, that each monk had to provide his own clothing, for each should receive money from the lord abbot for clothing and 'they should clearly declare what they have spent the money on'.

This part of the report suggests that private money and 'the vice of private ownership' were common at Rufford at this time. This property must have included not just money, jewellery and vessels of gold or silver, but weapons (no doubt partly for hunting) including bows and arrows and two-edged swords; animals - horses, cows, sheep - and fixed property - fields, woods, tithes. All of these were listed by the Visitors as unacceptable, 'nor should anyone call anything his own or believe it so'.

The report makes no mention of any particular scandal, but is much concerned about its possibility. 'All the doors of the cells in the dormitory should be completely removed ... and there should be diligent inspection every night and midday (when the monks were also required to rest) of the beds of every person'. Absence either as a fugitive or 'in the contagion of the flesh' was to be severely punished. Women unless they were 'ladies, princesses or the wives of knights' were to be wholly excluded from the monastic enclosure, 'for entries and loitering of this sort could be harmful to the monastery'. But there was a problem. The abbot had granted residence to a number of women, no doubt in return for payment or endowments, and he 'must now hasten to expel anyone dwelling here if he is at all able to do so'. In future no woman of any condition was to be permitted to stay in the monastery.

Punishment for breaking the rules was severe, imprisonment, beating and a diet of bread and water were the norm, unless the offender 'asks pardon from his heart and promises to mend his ways'. For less pardonable sins, such as talking to anyone of a bad reputation or a dissolute woman within the monastic enclosure, excommunication was ordained. In this the Cistercians seem to have been much stricter than some other Orders, where even adulterous priors seem to have suffered little punishment.

On a more positive note, the abbot was to provide a properly qualified schoolmaster to teach the youngsters the foundations of grammar. They were to speak only Latin at certain times and get used to writing it. The clever ones were to be sent to Oxford for higher studies according to the resources of the monastery; the less capable should apply themselves to scripture or the binding of codices. The abbot was also to provide a room in the infirmary (presumably for the poor) 'furnished with beds and utensils, where the sick and weak who do not usually have rooms may be received charitably' and looked after by 'diligent servants' deputed for this work. The abbot 'should minister to the sick with real fatherly solicitude'.

As regards administration, officials were to render a full set of accounts every month, while that abbot 'in the presence of the wiser part of the convent' was to provide a statement of the monastery's finances so that 'the House of God may be governed in a wise way by wise persons'. Again, this suggests the need to tighten procedures rather than any major problem.

The Dissolution

Rufford was visited by Layton and Legh in 1536. They often found spurious reasons why a monastery should be closed: here their report claimed - most probably incorrectly - that the abbot had been incontinent with two married and four single women. In addition, six of the fifteen monks were said to desire exemption from their vows. No evidence of any opposition to closure is recorded and the abbey was duly dissolved. In spite of official doubts about his chastity, Abbot Thomas Doncaster was given a pension of £25 a year. But he soon relinquished this on his appointment to the important rectory of Rotherham, which had belonged to the abbey for 300 years. The fate of the other monks is not known though it has been suggested by Professor Claire Cross that some of them may have continued to meet, thus perpetuating for a while their social and religious life.

Later History

The abbey buildings and demesne land, comprising 304 acres of arable, 640 of pasture and 60 of meadow, were originally leased to Sir John Markham of Ollerton. But the next year Henry VIII granted them to George Talbot, Earl of Shrewsbury, for help in crushing the Pilgrimage of Grace. He was succeeded by the sixth Earl in 1560, and it is his wife, Bess of Hardwick, who is said to have altered the lay brothers' quarters into a house. Much of the rest of the abbey was demolished by 1650.

In the early seventeenth century the house was searched many times following reports that the then Countess Mary, an ardent Catholic, was hiding papists. But none was ever found. In 1620 the estate passed to the Savile family. Even towards the end of the century the Elizabethan house still made a desirable home, for in 1680 Sir George Savile wrote, 'Poor old Rufford with all its wrinkles hath more charms for me than London can show'.[2] Sir George, later Lord Halifax, was known as 'the Trimmer' on account of his political gyrations. He extended the house, and the family continued to add to the estate, so that eventually it included an orangery, ornamental canal, formal gardens, a lake and a mill, and even one of England's first swimming pools.

Further additions were made in the 1820s by the architect Anthony Salvin, including a Tudor-style entrance porch and a clock tower. But in 1938 high taxes forced the sale of the estate. The house was largely demolished in 1956, but parts of the original abbey buildings still survive including the lay brothers' frater, one of the best preserved in England.

References

1. C.J. Holdsworth (ed.), *Rufford Charters* vol. 3, Thoroton Society Record Series, xxxii, (1980), no: 1004, 555-61

2. *Savile Correspondence*, Camden Society 71, (1858), 134

Access

OS 646647. The site lies 2 miles south of Ollerton, just off the A614. The estate is owned by Nottinghamshire County Council and is a popular park and craft centre. The house and abbey remains are cared for by English Heritage and are in part open to the public.

Shelford Priory

Sue Terry and John Hamilton

helford parish lies in the narrow Trent floodplain, just back from the east bank of the river a few miles downstream from Nottingham. The village was noted in Domesday as having a priest and a church and as being mostly in the fee of Goisford de Halselin. Since no foundation charter survives, the circumstances and date of the priory's foundation can only be inferred from a dispute over patronage which arose in 1258 between two local landowners. From this it emerged that both Ralph Halselin and Robert de Caus had endowed the priory in the reign of Henry II, but Ralph was confirmed as the founder, having 'enfeoffed it of all his lands in Shelford and divers other lands'. Robert de Caus was not forgotten, however, for in 1534 alms were still being paid daily for the foundation of the priory by Ralph Halselin and Robert Caus, 'founders of the aforesaid house'.

Whatever the exact date, the priory was established in the middle years of the twelfth century as a house of canons regular of St Augustine. This was in spite of the presence of the much larger Thurgarton priory only half a dozen miles away, also an Augustinian house - but Augustinian monasteries were the cheapest to establish. It was sited in open countryside close to the river, but nearly a mile from the village. Nearby was Gunthorpe ferry, for access to which the monks were able to extract 3s annually from their brethren at Thurgarton.

The priory was only modestly endowed from the start, although apart from the Halselin lands in Shelford, the original endowment included various churches with part at least of the churches of Gedling just across the river and of Westborough and Doddington in Lincolnshire.

Architectural History

Today the priory, or Shelford Manor as it is now called, is a private house. It is built of ashlar and dressed coarse rubble, and incorporates masonry from the original monastic buildings. But in the absence of archaeological investigation it has not been possible to establish the site plan or layout of the priory buildings. The ground to the front of the manor house is very uneven and suggests foundations may lie underneath. There is also evidence of medieval foundations in the cellars of the present house; and some medieval stonework, perhaps from the priory cloisters, has been incorporated into gate and wall constructions in the now unused west entrance to the manor. The only documentary evidence of building activity is an instruction from Archbishop Giffard to his bailiff in Southwell in 1270 to supply three oaks for timber for the priory. By the early fourteenth century the buildings were substantial enough to accommodate Edward II and his entourage.

Economic History

Shelford was always one of the smaller Nottinghamshire monasteries. This was particularly so in the early years; in 1291 its taxable income of £65 was only a quarter of that of Thurgarton. Nevertheless, there was a slow accumulation of property, much of it in Shelford itself and nearby villages. In 1230, for example, Archbishop Gray confirmed pensions to the priory from the churches of Burton Joyce, Gedling and Laxton, as well as a stone of wax from Kelham.

The pace of acquisition increased in the fourteenth century. The churches of Shelford and Saxondale and part of the church at North Muskham were acquired in 1310-11. A few years later Edward II granted the priory a licence to purchase property to the value of £20. In 1348 the priory acquired the church of Burton Joyce; and in the 1390s more property was added both locally and in Derbyshire and Lincolnshire. These new sources of income were as likely to be the result of purchase or exchange as through gifts or legacies. Proportionately the priory was one of the most successful in the county in raising its income after 1291, more than doubling it by 1535. But at £152 gross this remained well below the average of Nottinghamshire houses. That the increase in income cannot by any means all be attributed to inflation is shown by the comparison of the handful of priory-owned properties listed by the *Taxatio* with the *Valor's* list of 39 parishes in which the priory had some stake in 1535.

The *Valor* also allows us to analyse its sources of income. Over half - some £74 after immediate deductions for such items as ecclesiastical dues - came from tithes from ten parishes: the local parishes of Shelford, Saxondale, Gedling and Burton Joyce produced £29, Elvaston in Derbyshire £23 alone, and Westborough in Lincolnshire, part of the priory's original endowment, more than £9. Next in importance at £29 came rents from land mainly in nearby villages, although the largest single amount again came from Elvaston. Nearly all the balance of £25 came from the priory's own farms. In 1537, these were described as comprising some 264 acres - two-thirds of it arable and the rest pasture and meadow - together with the common and fishery, and some woodland. Sheep farming for wool was certainly carried out in the fourteenth century, but otherwise we have no certain information on the priory's farming activities.

Monastic Life

Evidence for the religious life of the priory is sparse and provides only tantalising glimpses of a small Augustinian community. Indeed the report by Layton and Legh on the eve of the Dissolution is perhaps the most important source we have. They present a picture of corruption and superstition, for they found:

> three sodomites, three guilty of incontinence, three desire release from religion. They venerate the girdle and milk of St Mary and part of a candle which it is believed she carried at her purification; they also have the oil of the Holy Cross and the oil of St Katherine.[1]

While the charges of sexual impropriety must be treated with scepticism, the report suggests a minimum of six canons at that time. The exact number at any time is unknown, but is unlikely ever to have exceeded a dozen.

The position of Shelford beside the river Trent and midway between the two ferries of Shelford and Gunthorpe may well have resulted in demands for hospitality from travellers, but there is no direct evidence for this. On the other hand, the relics kept by the priory suggest that it had a reputation for pilgrimage and medical care. The girdle of St Mary was associated with pregnancy and childbirth to ease labour and ensure a healthy child, while the oils may have been held to have had healing powers for sores and wounds.

In their report Layton and Legh failed to mention the almshouses maintained by the priory to support six poor men, as noted at the Dissolution, though it is not known how long they had existed before that time. Neither do they make note of the distribution of 'broken meats' which the priory would almost certainly have made, as Lady Stanhope did after them. In 1280 Archbishop Romayne at his Visitation ordered that 'old clothes ... be given to the poor without payment ... the sick to be better fed and tended'. He also tells the prior to temper his indulgence in drink, but his other injunctions suggest no other serious problem at that time. In 1280 too there is mention of 'the canons' boys returning from their exterior labour', but no other evidence for a school exists. The public records, however, provide evidence of the Crown's use of priors of Shelford to stop unwanted tournaments in the thirteenth century and to oversee the local collection of taxes in the fourteenth. King Edward II also twice made use of the priory's hospitality, staying there in 1317 and 1319. But the general absence of information about Shelford suggests a small monastery modestly living out a continuing life of quiet religion.

The Dissolution

In death as in life, Shelford Priory seems to have behaved as a typical modest religious house, only slightly enlivened by the brief involvement of the doomed Henry Norris. In October 1520 Norris, 'Squire of the Body' of Henry VIII, was granted the patronage of the priory together with the lordships of the manors of Shelford and several other local villages. By the time Layton and Legh came in 1536 on their notorious Visitation, Norris was dead, attainted for alleged involvement with Queen Anne Boleyn. Shelford was one of the smaller religious houses included in the first series of these audits, the visitors finding an income of £100 and debts of £30, both suspiciously round figures, although the income figure is reasonably close to the more detailed *Valor* one of £117 net. These sums do not suggest the priory was in serious financial difficulty. On the religious side, Layton and Legh were bent on finding two sorts of evidence to support closure: personal misconduct and superstition. As noted above, they reported finding both; but the relics were not mentioned in their report. With their indication of medical care and the priory's almshouses, these showed concern for the poor and both suggest there was more in the way of Christian activity at the priory than the investigators cared to admit.

The actual break-up of the religious community appears to have taken place quietly, probably in 1536. Robert Dixon, the last prior, was granted £16 in what seems to have been a one-off payment. Miles Holme, the only other known pensioner, was still being paid £3 14s 0d *per annum* in 1556.

Later History

After the Dissolution, Archbishop Cranmer made an unsuccessful plea for the site on behalf of his brother-in-law. He wrote to Cromwell, 'I desire your favour for the bearer, my brother-in-law, who is now clerk of my kitchen, to have the farm of the priory of Shelford'.[2] Perhaps Cromwell felt he owed the archbishop no favours or was seeking the support of a person of greater political weight than a 'clerk to the kitchen'. In the event it was Sir Michael Stanhope and his wife who obtained the grant to the lands and eventually all the assets of the priory. Stanhope was the second son of Sir Edward and Lady Adeline Stanhope of Rampton. His stepsister Anne married Edward, Duke of Somerset, later Protector to the boy-King Edward VI. This connection led to Stanhope's execution for treason and the temporary loss of the Shelford lands by the family. But the Stanhopes, subsequently Earls of Chesterfield, later regained control of them.

Life for the local community appears to have been little changed by the Dissolution. The estate was run much as before, there being no evidence of change to tenancy agreements, entry fines or enclosure. Lady Anne Stanhope

continued the charitable relief of the poor. As to the buildings, little is known of any construction or alteration before 1600, but around this time work was carried out for the Stanhopes by one of the Smithsons, either father or son, famous for their work on Wollaton Hall.

View of the site showing the proximity of the priory to the river Trent

During the Civil War the Stanhopes were Royalists and in 1645 the manor house was attacked by Parliamentary forces. Colonel Philip Stanhope and several of his soldiers were killed, the house taken by storm and burned to the ground. A stonemason working on the building in recent times noted that the stone in the east corner of the room now used as a kitchen had at some point been subjected to great heat, evidence perhaps that the original stone was *in situ* or perhaps had been re-used in the rebuilding of 1678. It is also just possible that the magnificent fireplace in the manor house dining room dates from the time of the priory; but it may have been relocated from elsewhere. The house was much altered and modernised during the nineteenth and twentieth centuries.

References

1. *Letters and Papers of Henry VIII, 10 1536*, 138, ref. 364

2. *Ibid.*, 215, ref. 547

Access

OS 673434. The Manor house built on the site of the priory is private property. It stands on its own and can be seen from the minor road between Gunthorpe bridge (A6097) and Shelford village.

Welbeck Abbey

Les Green and David Bewley

The first Premonstratensian house in England was founded at Newhouse in Lincolnshire in 1143 and Welbeck was one of the eleven daughter houses established from there during the following 70 years. Founded in 1153, Welbeck in turn established another seven houses in a 40-year period of great fervour and activity. Sponsored by Thomas de Flemmaugh of Cuckney, a grandson of one of William the Conqueror's followers, Welbeck was built on a gentle east-facing slope above the river Poulter. Thomas, described as being 'a most warlike man', supported Stephen against the claims of Queen Matilda and had built a church and motte and bailey castle commanding a ford on the Poulter. Work in the 1950s on the church foundations revealed a mass grave; was this a relic of some long forgotten disaster and a possible reason for the foundation of Welbeck as an act of atonement? The Premonstratensian canons were a preaching order and thus able to supply priests to serve the churches they were given. In return, they were entitled to collect the tithes, rents and other dues from the parishes. Over the years Welbeck acquired ten churches and two chapels, but by the end of the fifteenth century was supplying canons as parish priests in only six of them. These canons in the parishes were expected to wear their habits and observe the monastic rule as far as possible. In 1512 Welbeck was declared the principal house of the Premonstratensian Order in England and Wales.

Architectural History

Welbeck Abbey was built on forest land about two miles north of Cuckney, just off the road to Worksop. The remains of this twelfth-century building are to be found in the basement of the present house, where the only recognisable features are a divided undercroft 100 feet long

and 25 feet wide with octagonal columns down the centre, together with a doorway which originally gave access to the cloister through the six-foot thick wall. This undercroft, the domain of the cellarer, was originally at ground level and remained so until the eighteenth century when, for aesthetic reasons, the ground level around the house was raised to first floor level. Immediately above the undercroft were the abbot's quarters with access to the church and cloister by means of an internal spiral stair. By the fifteenth century there was an imposing external entrance to the abbot's rooms for the use of visitors by way of a tower and stone stairs.

By taking the undercroft as a starting point, by observing angles and positions of other features, by reference to a plan of 1750 and by dowsing the external site, it has been possible to reconstruct a ground plan of the abbey. The general layout was conventional, with the cloister to the south of the church. The remains of the church and the south and east ranges of the cloister buildings are now buried beneath formal gardens and not accessible for excavation. The church, dedicated to St James, was very large with north and south aisles and a central tower. The indications are that the church was some 286 feet long and 65 feet wide and compares closely with Southwell Minster built 50 years earlier and measuring 308 feet by 63 feet.

Economic History

At its foundation, Welbeck received income from land and churches in the immediate vicinity of the abbey and from other churches in Derbyshire and Lincolnshire. It soon acquired rights to quarry at Whitwell and to the churches at Flintham, Whatton, Bothamsall, Elkesley and a part share in the church at Kelham. Land rights at North Wingfield and Peak Forest in Derbyshire were added to those at Duckmanton, Newbold and Cresswell. The *Taxatio* of Pope Nicholas in 1291 records a taxable income of £112 divided equally between spiritualities and temporalities. The fourteenth century saw a rapid increase in this, for within two years Welbeck's income rose to £140 by the acquisition of the rectories at Littleborough, Etwall, Whitton, Coates and Duckmanton. Income was also derived from the sale of wool, recorded in the fourteenth century and later coal in the fifteenth century.

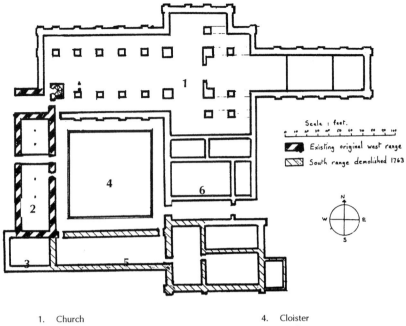

Scale : feet.

▨ Existing original west range
▧ South range demolished 1763

N
W ✛ E
S

1. Church
2. Undercroft with Abbot's quarters over
3. Entrance to Abbot's rooms
4. Cloister
5. South range
6. East range

Suggested plan of monastic buildings based on metal rod dowsing

In 1329 the abbey was granted the manor of Cuckney, together with seven nearby hamlets. In return, the abbey agreed to provide eight canons to celebrate mass daily for the health and welfare of Edward III, his Queen and ancestors and also for Piers Gaveston, the late King's favourite, and finally for the Bishop of Ely who had arranged the grant. This commitment Welbeck swore to maintain for ever, a point which was later presented as a legal reason why the abbey could not be dissolved. However, this objection was overruled.

The *Valor Ecclesiasticus* of 1535 showed Welbeck as a comparatively wealthy house with an income of £298 gross, £249 net, of which 45 per cent derived form spiritualities and 55 per cent from temporalities. Part of this income came from the fact that Welbeck was now the principal house of the Premonstratensian order in England and Wales and the abbot held the office of Visitor General. This brought in £14 annually plus a further £14 10s 0d levied every four years at a General Chapter. Included in the

outgoings was £8 13s 4d expended in obligatory alms, namely 3s 4d to the poor of Anstey on Good Friday and the remainder in ale and bread weekly at the abbey. This alms-giving accounted for just 3.4 per cent of the total income.

Monastic Life

Before the late fifteenth century there is little extant information on the daily life of the abbey. But one, clearly unusual, incident occurred in 1393. It concerned a violent attack by the canons, their servants and men from the nearby village of Norton and illustrates the close involvement of the abbey in everyday life outside its walls. The incident is recorded in the Patent Rolls on 11 February 1393 with a royal pardon to the persons involved:

Pardon to William Broun of Norton by Welbeck of suit of the King's peace for felonies, treasons and other offences under the following circumstances:

Visitation Dates at Welbeck Abbey			
1475	31 May 1478	1482	23 May 1488
Willelmus Burton, Abbot (1473) Robertus Stanley, Prior Ricardus Symondson, Sub-prior Johannes Clevyn, Vicar of Litilburgh Johannes Beauchef, Vicar of Whatton[1]	Abbot Prior[3] Chaplain near to Bothusell Vicar of Lytilburgh Vicar of Whatton	Abbot[4] Not listed, at Bothumsall Not listed, at Whatton	Johannes Ackaster, Abbot[9]
Robertus Forest, Vicar of Cuckney Johannes Warburton, Circator Thomas Halom, no office Robertus Awstyn, Provisor exteriorum[2] Willelmus Bradforde, Succentor	Vicar of Cuckney Circator In hospital Magistrum grangie, Officarius in Pistrino Custos grangie	Vicar of Cuckney No office No office No office No office[5]	No office[10]
Johannes Colby, no office Ricardus Holynbryg, no office Johannes Lancaster, no office Johannes Myrst, Chaplain in Whatton Ricardus Cambrige, Vicar of Cotes	Provisor exteriorum Sub-prior No office Chaplain near to Aslacton Vicar of Cotes	Sacrist and Circator[6] Sub-prior No office No office Not listed[7]	Vicar of Cuckney[11] No office Vicar of Cotes Vicar of Whitton (Whatton)[12]
Thomas Laxton, no office Ricardus Rolston, Novice Christoferas Hessyl, Novice Johannes Urslet, Cantor Johannes Wentbryg, Sacrist	Cellarer Deacon Deacon Cantor Sacrist	Assistant (Cuckney) Not listed Near to Whitton (Whatton)[5] Cantor Not listed	Sub-prior No office[13] Cellarer Cantor Chaplain at Bothumsell
Thomas Derby, Vicar of Wytton	Vicar of Whitton Johannes Ray, Novice Succentorem Willelmus Swan, Novice	Not listed at Whitton Prior[8] Chaplain Wyllemus Hankyn, no office Robertus Sharppe, Novice	Vicar of Whatton (Whitton) Vicar of Lytyllburgh Vicar of Whitton[14] Sacrist
		Johannes Nicholsone, Novice	Not listed Willelmus Stow, Sub-Sacrist Edwardus Colynson, Sub-deacon Thomas Wilkynson, Refectory and novices Ricardus Colle, Succentor diaconius

1. Inducted 7 May 1447 at Whatton
2. Excused attendance at chair due to age and infirmity 7 May 1472
3. Summoned to Doncaster to answer unspecified charges 16 August 1478
4. Deposed for numerous offences. Sentenced to detention at Barlings Abbey, commuted? Instituted vicar of Cuckney 18 November 1483
5. Both found guilty of incontinence, apostasy and rebellion
6. Appointed temporary Abbot 1482. Instituted Vicar of Cuckney on death of W. Burton 16 October 1484
7. Instituted Vicar of Whatton 19 November 1484
8. Very rapid advancement in unsettled times
9. Former Abbot of Tupholme (LIncs) 1475-82
10. Transferred to Sulby 1488 and became Cellarer 1494-1500
11. Ordered to pay annual fee of 20s for his meals in Welbeck
12. Whatton. Instituted 19 November 1484
13. Guilty of incontinence with Emma Spedman. Forty days bread and water
14. Guilty of disobedience. Forty days bread and water
15. Became Abbot of Newbo 21 January 1492
16. Became Vicar of Cuckney January 1493
17. Guilty of disobedience, absence and hunting. Given one year to learn psalter by heart

18. Instituted Vicar of Cuckney January 1492. Died January 1493
19. Punished for eating meat at home of laity near the abbey
20. Canon of Welford sent to Welbeck in punishment 17 January 1488. Guilty of disobedience, sent to St Agatha for 10 years 14 August 1491. Licensed to proceed to Oxford or Cambridge at his family's expense 30 April 1492
21. Former Abbot of Beaucheffe (Sheffield) from 1482
22. Transferred to Beaucheffe. Instituted Vicar of Wemswalde (Wymswold)
23. Excommunicated for apostasy. Absented himself but surrendered at Torre Abbey, Devon 12 June 1494, 40 days punishment followed by three years strict imprisonment at Welbeck
24. Punished for non-regulation tonsure
25. Instituted 5 March 1495
26. Instituted Vicar of Whatton 24 November 1503
27. Temporary abbot 1502. Vicar of Cuckney 1506
28. Notorious for disorderly life and debts. Promised to reform
29. Instituted Vicar of Whatton 18 March 1499. Elected abbot 1503. Appointed Commisory General and Visitor for the Order 1505

Visitation Dates at Welbeck Abbey			
14 August 1491	29 May 1494	3 September 1497	22 November 1500
Abbot	Thomas Wyder, Abbot[21]	Thomas Widdur, Abbot	Thomas Wyddour, Abbot
Vicar of Cokney[15] No office Vicar of Cotes Not listed	[22] Vicar of Cotes Vicar of Whattone	 Vicar of Whittone (Whatton)	
Sub-prior No office No office Cantor Vicar of Bothumsalle	Near to Cuckney Not listed Cellarer Near Whattone Vicar of Bodomschalle	Supporter (Cuckney) Licentiate Cellarer Supporter (Whatton) Vicar of Bothumsalle[24]	 Cellarer[26] Supporter (Cuckney) Vicar of Bothumsalle
Vicar of Whittone Vicar of Lytylborow[16] No office[17] Circator	Vicar of Whittone Vicar of Cukney Chaplain Circator	Vicar of Whattone (Whitton) Vicar of Cukney No office Chaplain	Vicar of Whattone (Whitton) Vicar of Cukney, died 1506 Chaplain No office[27]
No office[18] Deacon[19] No office Sacrist Succentor	 Vicar of Lytylburghe No office[23] Sub-prior Sacrist	 No office Vicar of Cotes[24,25] Prior Circator	 Licentiate Vicar of Lytylburghe[28] Vicar of Whittone (Whatton)[29]
Ricardus Gylyot, no office Robertus Thorntone, no office Nicholaus Lylborne, Novice Johannes Styrtyll, Novice Ricardus Junkyne, Vicar of Whattone	Novice Novice Cantor Succentor	Succentor No office Sub-prior Sacrist	No office No office Prior
Robertus Flescher, Cellarer Edwardus Seyton, not listed[20]	Robertus Otlay, Sub-cellarer Willelmus Hornby, Novice Johannes Seniore, Novice	Vicar of Lytilburgh No office Novice	Sub-cellarer Circator Sub-prior
	Johannes Kuk, Novice	Novice	Sub-Sacrist Ricardus Cuke, Novice Nicholas Wydour, Novice Thomas Avrwyk, Novice sub-deacon

Table 4

Names of the community of Welbeck

Robert Veel, keeper of the rolls of the King's Bench, and John Wynchecombe, appointed by the king to take carts for the carriage of the rolls, being directed on Saturday before the feast of St Katherine last by Walter Clopton, Chief Justice, and the other justices to carry the said rolls from York to Nottingham by Tuesday then following, were proceeding therein when, owing to the excessive rainfall affecting the roads, they could not without additional horses reach Nottingham, whereupon by virtue of their commission and the justices' order they took at Norton (one and a half miles south of Welbeck) aforesaid two horses of John Levet and John Turnour of Norton, to be paid for in due course. Thereupon the said William Broun, John Northeryn, Robert Bocher, all of Norton, and Hugh Mat, servant of John Baukwell, Abbot of Welbeck, with divers other evildoers came armed with bows and arrows, sticks and swords, and at dusk of the same day raised all the men of Norton in insurrection, pursued the said Robert and John to Warsop (three miles south of Norton) and instigated by Simon de Castelton, canon of Welbeck, and John Worsop, vicar of Cuckney (and canon of Welbeck), assulted them, shot at and pierced the books in the carriage and took the horses, and would have carried the same away but that by the grace of God and their help they made too good a defence.

The like (pardon) the said John Northeryn, Robert Bocher and Hugh Mat, servant of John Baukwell, Abbot of Welbeck.[1]

Apart from seeking confirmation from the local bishop for the appointment of their canons to act as parish priests, the Premonstratensians were a self-regulating body and were exempt from all diocesan control.

Regulation was by means of the triennial Visitation, the procedure for which was clearly laid down. The Visitor first informed the abbey of his impending visit, giving the date well in advance. Canons resident in parishes were to be recalled, books and accounts made available for inspection and the annual levies ready for his collection. On arrival, he held a formal meeting in the chapter house, at which he explained the meaning and purpose of the Visitation and the obligation that all present had to disclose anything which might need correction. No-one was to accuse his superior without having previously informed him of his intention; no-one was to be accused of faults committed before the previous Visitation unless new knowledge had been obtained since then; no-one was to propose correction of anything already legislated for. The Visitor then checked that ecclesiastical customs were being observed, prayers for the founders said, and novices properly instructed and presented. After this meeting he held individual interviews with all the members of the community from the abbot down. In the case of a serious charge being laid, he held a legal inquiry with other brethren acting as a jury. Punishment was meted out where necessary and the findings were publicised and recorded. It appears that many sentences were commuted because of intercession by fellow brethren and this, too, he recorded in his reports.

For the last quarter of the fifteenth century we are fortunate in having available records of the Visitations of all Premonstratensian houses including Welbeck. This is due to the work of Bishop Richard Redman, a most zealous and energetic man. He was abbot of the small house at Shap in Westmorland in 1459, appointed Visitor of the Order's houses in 1478, and successively Bishop of St Asaph, Exeter and Ely while still retaining his abbacy of Shap. He attempted to visit each house personally once every three years, travelling from Shap as far afield as Torre in Devon, Talley in Carmarthen and Langdon near Dover.

On the occasion of his first visit to Welbeck Bishop Redman planned the final stage of his journey carefully. He first wrote to the Abbot of Welbeck on 11 September giving notice of his impending visit on 9 December following. In his letter he ordered that all canons, both in the abbey and in the outlying parishes, should be present at the time of his visitation and that the annual subsidies of 66s 8d *per annum* due from the time of the last visitation be ready for his collection. He also ordered that dinner should be prepared for himself and his attendants at the village of Papplewick and that he should then be escorted from there to Welbeck in time for supper. The meal at Papplewick was to be at Welbeck's expense and the messenger carrying his letter was to have his expenses paid in addition to being suitably rewarded. Papplewick lies about eight miles north of Nottingham and Welbeck is a further thirteen miles to the

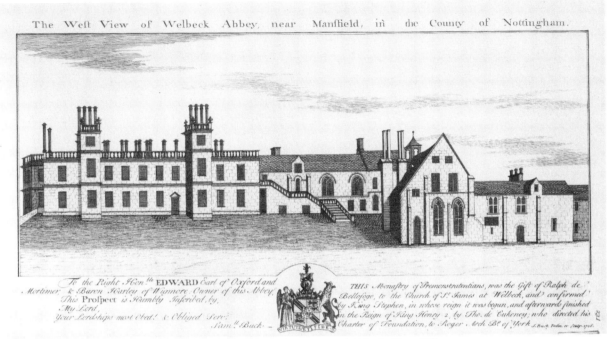

The West View of Welbeck Abbey, near Mansfield, in the County of Nottingham.

Samuel Buck's engraving of the west view of Welbeck Abbey, 1726

north. Dinner at midday in the depths of winter would leave few daylight hours for the journey through the densest part of Sherwood Forest passing the priory at Newstead and the Cistercian abbey of Rufford before arriving at Welbeck. One must admire his courage and determination in undertaking such a journey at that time of year.

When Bishop Redman found things satisfactory, as he did in most cases, he merely said they are satisfactory and did not elaborate. It is only the faults and offences that we find mentioned in his reports. Non-attendance at services, especially Matins - the first service of the day at 2am - was frequently reported, as were infringements of standards of dress and appearance. The wearing of slippers was banned and at Lavendon Abbey, Buckinghamshire, the canons were given fourteen days to have their tunics lengthened down to their knees. An inclination to wear black tunics instead of white was outlawed by a general decree on the grounds that the Premonstratensians then became indistinguishable from the Augustinians. The wearers of strange tonsures were punished by being put on bread and water as were those guilty of disobedience.

Despite vows of poverty, Premonstratensian canons retained some control over personal financial matters. Those out in parishes had the income from their livings on which to support themselves, while the canon in charge at Cuckney was close enough to Welbeck to return there for some of his meals, for which he had to pay 20s *per annum*. It was also possible for canons to get into debt, one being ordered to discharge his debt before the next General Chapter (held every four years). Several times Bishop Redman ordered abbots to pay their canons the 'usual' 20s *per annum* for their clothes. He did not say where they should spend this money to purchase their garments.

The bishop was aware that a good standard of food was important for the well-being of a community and several times he ordered that improvements should be made. On the other hand, the diet had to be kept within regulation limits.

At a Provincial Chapter at Lincoln in 1495 the following ordinance was issued:

It having been brought to their notice that some eat eggs and *lacticinia* at supper on Mondays and Wednesdays and others fish and *lacticinia* both at dinner and supper, the practice was condemned and it was decreed that in all houses on those days flesh should be eaten twice as on other days except in Lent and Advent and on other days when forbidden to the Universal Church. No supper on Saturdays.[2]

Lacticinium is defined as being 'whytmete', probably chicken. Flesh to be eaten twice a day comes as something of a surprise and hints that the late fifteenth century monastic regime was perhaps not quite as austere as we might have thought. Bishop Redman also found it necessary to issue warnings about eating and drinking outside the abbey without permission and insisted that canons have their meals within the abbey as a community.

At Newbo Abbey, near Lincoln, the bishop recommended recreation 'twice a week and on Sundays', but did not specify the nature of this recreation. We do know the types of activity he deplored. There was to be no hunting in the woods; no games of cards or dice for money, and at Torre Abbey, Devon he banned tennis - especially when played for money - further indications that the canons had money at their disposal. The tennis must have been real (or royal) tennis, for which the cloister area with its sloping roof over the cloister walk would have been an ideal setting. The fact that they played this type of tennis hints at the aristocratic background of some of the canons, for this game was evolved and played at the royal court.

Some aspects of life, however, are never or hardly ever mentioned. There is no reference to scholarship or training and only once did he refer to work when he enjoined the canons of Torre Abbey to 'undertake work in gardens and harvest willingly'. There is only one reference to lay brothers and boys, again at Torre, when he ordered that 'seculars are not to eat with brethren either in the infirmary or the refectory, nor are they to be present at their conferences, drinking or recreations except certain boys appointed by the abbot'.

As one might expect in a community such as Welbeck, disobedience, 'rebellion', and apostasy occurred from time to time along with lapses in sexual behaviour, few being as serious as the case of Abbot Burton. William Burton was elected abbot around 1473 and soon showed his disregard of authority by setting out, without permission, to visit Leiston Abbey in Suffolk, one of Welbeck's daughter houses. He took with him ten horsemen and stayed for eight days at the abbey's expense. By 1478 things had begun to deteriorate at Welbeck and an inspection notes that the monastic rule should be more closely observed, that sick quarters and better food needed to be providing, and that repairs were needed to the fabric of the house. Hunting in the woods and other 'wanton pursuits' should cease. The abbey was reported to be in debt for £90 and not properly provisioned.

At the time of the next inspection, in 1482, matters could no longer be concealed and Abbot Burton was accused of 'dreadful dishonesty' and of ruining his own reputation and that of the abbey:

He has squandered the abbey's goods both movable and immovable, allowed the buildings to collapse through want of repair and let out land and tithes to local rich men. He has sold timber and all the oxen and sheep and pawned the abbey's plate leaving not one silver dish or salt cellar to place before guests. Even the abbey's services have suffered, there being no candles, oil or wine without which it is impossible to celebrate Mass. All this he has done in order to finance his gambling which he carries on night and day in the company of disreputable people. In addition he is living with several women in fornicating relationships, out of which he has begotten several children who have been raised at the abbey's expense.[3]

Needless to say, he was relieved of his post and dispatched to Barlings Abbey in Lincolnshire for punishment. Surprisingly, Welbeck was left temporarily in the charge of one of its own canons and the final appointment given to yet another Welbeck man. After such a catalogue of wrongdoing one might have expected that a new broom from outside the abbey would have been brought in. In spite of the seriousness of his offences, we find that Abbot Burton's sentence of ten years exile must have been commuted. He was recorded as being recalled in November 1483, barely a year after his downfall and instituted as vicar of Cuckney, one of Welbeck's prime appointments and close to the abbey. He died in the following year.

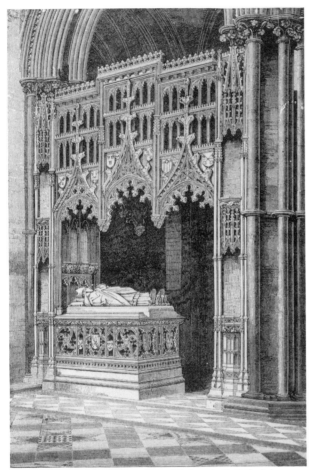

The monument of Bishop Richard Redman in Ely Cathedral

Redman recorded his visits in detail and compiled lists of the names and appointments of the canons in each house during most of his remarkable 27 years in office, enabling us to trace the careers of the men who entered the Order as novices. Widely differing career patterns are to be seen over the 25 years (see table 4). Some, like John Colby (1475), got to the top. After a short period as temporary Abbot of Welbeck, he moved to be vicar at Cuckney and was then promoted to be Abbot at Newbo (1492). Thomas Wilkynson (1488) became Prior by 1497, Abbot of Welbeck in 1503 and Commissary General and Visitor for

the Order in 1505. John Ray, novice in 1478, achieved rapid promotion to Prior by 1482, but then spent his remaining years as a vicar - at Littleborough for five years and then at Cuckney.

Others obviously found it difficult to abide by the strict rules of the Order. Edward Colynson was constantly in trouble; in 1494 he was excommunicated for breaking his vows. He ran away but then surrendered himself at Torre in Devon two weeks later and was sentenced to 40 days punishment on bread and water followed by three years' strict imprisonment back at Welbeck. This sentence must have been reduced, for less than a year later he was to be found at Coates church, well away from any supervision. In 1497 he was punished for having an unusual tonsure and in 1500 accused of being notorious for leading a disorderly life and for getting into debt, this after being transferred to even more remote Littleborough. It appeared, as in the case of the disreputable Abbot Burton, that the Premonstratensian Order was able to overlook such behaviour at times.

If we knew more about the family backgrounds of these men and what outside pressures were exerted upon the abbey to rehabilitate them, we might better understand how such situations came about. William Hankyn, while at Whitton in 1482, possibly as assistant to Thomas Derby, had an affair with Emma Speedman; he was brought back to the abbey and later found guilty of disobedience, absence and hunting. Then there was the case of Edward Seyton (1491) who obviously found that he was completely unsuited to the monastic life and was allowed to leave to attend university at his family's expense. On the other hand, Thomas Derby (1475) spent a quarter of a century at Whitton without any complaint being laid at his door. It is worth observing again that it was the miscreants who got special mention in the Visitation records and that the majority who complied and lead exemplary lives passed unnoticed.

Redman's records also enable us to ascertain the number of canons at Welbeck over this period, once allowance has been made for discrepancies. The churches of Whatton and Whitton are often confused in the reports and in 1482 several members were omitted only to reappear at the following Visitation. Throughout this period the total

---

Table 5

Extract from the Visitation Diary of Thomas Wilkinson - 1506

9	May	At same place (Coverham). Spent night at Wedderby (40 mile journey) expense of Abbot of Coverham.
10	May	At Pomfreth (20 miles) at hour of evening meal. Expense of Abbot of Beauchyff.
11	May	At Beaucheff (30 miles) at hour of evening meal.
12	May	Carried out visitation and same day completed.
13	May	Departed. At Dale (30 miles) at hour of evening meal.
14	May	The Visitation.
15	May	Departed. Spent night at Lichfield (32 miles). Expense of Abbot of Dale.
16	May	At Halesowen (20 miles) at hour of Vespers. Visitation same day.
17	May	Departed. (He does not say where he lodged that night.)
18	May	At Gloucester (50 miles from Halesowen). Expense of Abbot of Hales.
19	May	At Brystow (Bristol 34 miles). At own expense.
20	May	At Glassenbury. (25 miles)[4]

He then journeyed by way of Taunton (24 miles), Colverton (21 miles), to Exeter (12 miles), arrived on 23 May and concluded with 'thank God for his help'.

---

number of canons varied only between 20 and 26, including the abbot. These triennial Visitations necessitated a considerable amount of travelling and took between three and five months to accomplish. It is worth noting that on one Visitation the bishop travelled from Salisbury to Exeter, in two days, a distance of 90 miles, and 175 miles, in four days from Torre Abbey (Torquay) to London. The only year when a Visitation was due and did not happen was 1485, a year of turmoil and strife which saw the overthrow of Richard III at Bosworth - perhaps a bad time to be travelling through the land. It is strange that the Visitation was not just postponed for a year but left for a further three years. Perhaps Redman did carry out the work but the records have been lost.

With the exception of 1488, the Visitations were carried out in two sessions, one in the spring from the end of April and a second in the autumn from late August to November. The summer, from mid-June to mid-August, when one could reasonably have expected that road conditions and daylight hours were at their best, was not used for travelling. There was no regular order in which houses were visited, every circuit had some variations which necessitated taking a different route.

Thomas Wilkinson, the Visitor for 1506, kept a diary of his travels and it is from this source that we learn details of his route and timetable. Journeys which took more than one day and called for an overnight stay were noted and the expense of the lodging charged to the abbot of the nearest house, usually the one towards which he was travelling. Rarely was a house charged for more than one night's expenses. If the Visitor decided to deviate from the direct route for his own purposes or inclination, then he paid his own expenses. An exception to this rule was a visit to Walsingham while going from Wendling Abbey, near East Dereham, to the abbey at West Dereham, a diversion he charged to the Abbot of Wendling. Thomas also recorded four days at Basingstoke 'to the King, staying in the same place'.

In his diary, Thomas Wilkinson noted that he commenced his Visitation of the 'northern parts' at Kendal on 23 April, and that after inspecting the houses in Northumberland, Lancashire and Yorkshire, he journeyed south by way of Dale Abbey and Halesowen, Warwickshire, to arrive at Exeter on 23 May. He must have started out from Welbeck some time before 23 April and travelled to Kendal, a distance of over 140 miles, before beginning his work. On this northern tour he carried out nine Visitations and covered over 560 miles. He travelled on 23 days, an average of 25 miles a day. On 5 May he went from Blanchland Abbey on the Northumberland/Durham border, to St Agatha's at Richmond in Yorkshire, a distance of 40 miles through wild and sparsely populated country. He was obviously well pleased with this day's achievement for he wrote 'in truth, at St Agatha's at the hour of Vespers or thereabouts'.

Having reached Exeter, he stayed there until 8 September when he began his circuit of the 'southern parts'. Bishop Redman, Thomas Wilkinson's predecessor, was for a time both Abbot of Shap in Cumbria and Bishop of Exeter, two major preferments 550 miles apart! How well he managed to cope with both jobs is unclear, but having two bases, one in the north and the other in the south was an advantage in planning his Visitation journeys. It appears that Thomas Wilkinson must have inherited some arrangement whereby he stayed in Exeter for three and a half months. What he did during this time is not recorded.

During his tour of the southern parts, Thomas travelled on 44 out of the 68 days it took him to complete the circuit - two days out of every three. He covered 870 miles and visited and reported on 21 abbeys, all in the space of 68 days. In total during the year 1506 he travelled almost 1600 miles and counting Welbeck itself, Shap, where he must have lodged at the start of his northern tour, and Torre, which he would have visited during his stay in Exeter, he saw and reported on 33 houses. He only missed visiting Talley in Wales and two small 'cells' in Lancashire. He did, however, manage to include the two nunneries at Broadholm and Irford, houses which Bishop Redman usually missed. On his safe arrival back at Welbeck in November, Thomas concluded his diary by writing in a heartfelt manner 'returned to the monastery at Welbeck to satisfaction and delight'.

The Dissolution

The *Valor Ecclesiasticus* of 1535 showed Welbeck as a comparatively wealthy house, thus escaping the dissolution of the smaller monasteries in 1536. The Duke of Norfolk, acting as Henry VIII's representative, assembled his forces at Welbeck before proceeding to negotiate with the leaders of the Lincolnshire Rising and the Pilgrimage of Grace in October of that same year. Eventually on 20 June, 1538, Welbeck was surrendered to the Royal Commissioners, the abbot and canons receiving pensions or being confirmed in their vicarages. The church and conventual buildings were stripped of all valuable materials - roof lead, bells, glass, timber and fittings and left open to the elements. The whole complex and surrounding acres, plus land in nearby parishes, was sold to Richard Whalley of Shelford in 1539 for £500. He would have found the west range containing the abbot's quarters and the south range with kitchen and canons' accommodation still habitable and in reasonable order.

Later History

After changing hands several times, Welbeck was bought by the Earl of Shrewsbury in 1599 for Charles Cavendish, the son of his wife, 'Bess of Hardwick', by a previous marriage. Charles' son, William, became the Duke of Newcastle and commander of the king's armies in the north during the Civil War. Welbeck was fortified and changed hands several times during the Duke's absence. The church, the east and south ranges were demolished, the west range extended and a new south wing added to create the present house which became the home of the Dukes of Portland until the early part of the twentieth century. Welbeck is now an army college and not normally open to the public.

References

1. *Calendar of Patent Rolls 1391-96,* 218

2. F.A. Gasquet (ed.), *Collectanea Anglo-Premonstratensia* vol. I, Camden Society, 3rd series (1904-6), 173, ref.92

3. *Ibid.,* 184-5, ref.634

4. *Ibid.,* 193-4, ref.102

Access

OS 564743. The site lies 4 miles southwest of Worksop, off the A60. It is private property.

Felley Priory

Jean Reid

_____

The priory was founded in 1156 by Ralph Britto of Annesley, whose family had the lordship of Annesley after the Conquest. Ralph added several canons of the Augustinian Order to the hermitage already existing for a 'single devout man', Brother Robert. The hermitage had been situated in the lea of a south-facing hillside with a stream nearby, a mile or so from Annesley. The mutilated foundation charter shows only the dedication of the priory to God, the Virgin Mary, St Helen and Brother Robert. The priory was made subject to Worksop Priory of the same order with an annual payment of 10s. Following considerable acrimony with the parent house, however, Felley obtained its independence in 1260 on payment of 20s annually to Worksop.

A Cartulary, which appears to have been collated in the early sixteenth century and is now in the British Museum, does not record any specific foundation grants. It does, however, record early gifts: small parcels of land dotted about Nottinghamshire and Derbyshire. The latter included lands given by members of the Heriz family. Alice de Heriz married Sir William Chaworth of Annesley at the end of the fourteenth century, when the Heriz badge, a hedgehog, became part of the Chaworth coat of arms. In due course the Chaworth family was to become owners of Felley. The priory's most important possession in 1194, when a papal bull confirmed the foundation, was the church of Annesley. This was said to have been given by Reginald de Annesley, son of the founder. The grant was disputed, but the ownership by the priory was confirmed at a special hearing at St Mary's church in Nottingham in May 1311, at the request of the canons while the 'ancient evidences' were 'yet perfect'.

Architectural History

The present building on the site is a charming long, low, gabled private house. The central part dates to the sixteenth and seventeenth centuries while the stone foundations are

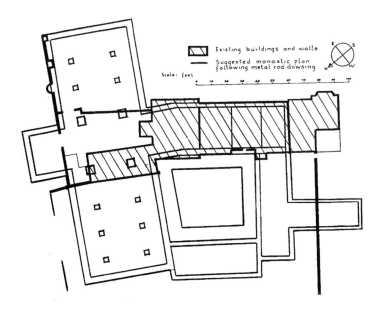

Plan of Felley Priory based on metal rod dowsing

probably part of the priory at the eastern end of the cloister. The present ground floor fireplace with its seventeenth-century chimney-stack, stands at the likely position of the priory warming-room. Dowsing indicated the cloister in the area of the present driveway of the house, this being surrounded by conventual buildings, including the church on the north side. The most visible of the priory's remains are four thirteenth century semicircular shafts with decorated capitals. They are not in their original position, but stand at the present courtyard and garden entrances. There are remains of buttresses on the south west corner of the newer north wing of the present house. If the plan

The present house on the site of the priory

of the church, suggested by the dowsing is correct, then these are likely to be part of a south transept. A bequest of land in 1248 for a daily Mass at the altar of St Edmund suggests that by then the church was large enough for at least one subsidiary altar. But scarcely twenty years later the priory was apparently so poverty-stricken that rain was coming through the roof. It may be assumed that considerable building was done in the mid-fourteenth century when the Close Rolls recorded four different gifts of wood from the royal forests. The present tall stone-capped and buttressed wall to the south may be part of the former priory boundary wall. Below the present house is a series of ponds, possibly once the priory fish ponds. Further to the south west was Felley Mill, but only the stream and 'race' survive. We can only assume this was the canons' mill.

Perhaps the most evocative survival from the priory is the beautiful lattice-patterned barrel-shaped Norman font which is now in Annesley parish church. This font was taken from the old and disused parish church where it would have been used by the canons when administering baptism.

Economic History

Further small grants of land were made in the thirteenth century by local landowners, such as Geoffrey de Langley and Geoffrey de Dethwick. These were usually attached to requests for masses either at the priory or at private chapels. One lot of sixteen acres together with smaller grants was given in 1203 by Serlo de Plessey, lord of Ashover, who had entered into fraternity with the convent. At the 1291 *Taxatio* the priory was the poorest in the county and tithes of small holdings in Sherwood Forest subsequently given under royal patent in 1305 were not enough to remove the financial burdens being experienced. Thus in 1343 the Archbishop of York allowed the appropriation of the church of Attenborough because of 'the barrenness of your lands, the impoverishment of your tenants, the repair ... of your buildings ... and the great weight of debt'. At this time Felley was valued at only £11 2s 0d, of which the church of Annesley was worth £5 6s 8d. Impoverishment continued and the Fine Rolls of the fifteenth century showed Felley as being exempt from payment of the tenth in time of storm and damage 'because of wretchedness and notorious poverty'.

Monastic Life

Felley Priory was never a large house: in 1276 there were the prior, three named canons and 'others'. With the acquisition of the church of Attenborough it was hoped to increase the numbers from five to nine regular canons. These canons were needed to say the daily Mass or Masses not only at the priory but also at churches or chapels for which they had a responsibility, such as Annesley or the little private chapel at Wandisly, near Selston. Where a bequest entailed a daily Mass further afield, as at Dethick, the prior would have had to find a secular priest - and pay him. Charitable duties of the priory were indicated by a bequest in 1268 for a loaf, a gallon of beer, and half a dish of meat to be given to thirteen poor people on the anniversary of the donor's death. A similar request, but for only five poor people, was to be given on the anniversary of his wife's death.

A sad picture is given of the priory at the time of the archiepiscopal Visitation in 1276, when Prior Ralph de Pleasley was deposed because of his lax and inefficient control: getting the house into debt, breaking the lock where the priory seal was kept against the wishes of the monks, manhandling a fellow canon, not involving himself in the services and being deemed unfit because 'of infirmity and senility'. At the same time three canons including the sub-prior were named for immorality. They included William of Dunham, who it was stated had a son by one Rosa; William had stolen from the priory in order to give to her and had relapsed 'into sin as a dog returns to its vomit'. In contrast, in 1302 the prior was deputed by the Archbishop to oversee the accounts of the nearby Augustinian house of Newstead, while two later priors went on to become priors of Worksop.

A description of the election of a new prior survives. The day after the deposition of Ralph de Pleasley the canons met for a solemn celebration of Mass. They then proceeded to the Chapter House singing the *Veni Creator*. After discussion they voted unanimously for Thomas de Wathenowe, who was led to the high altar to the chanting of the *Te Deum* and ringing of bells. There he prostrated himself and kissed the altar. The next day at Southwell the Archbishop, continuing on his Visitation, gave his consent to the election.

The Dissolution

Alone of all the Nottinghamshire houses, Felley had no adverse report after the Cromwellian Visitation of 1535. At the time of the *Valor Ecclesiasticus* the priory was valued at £61 gross, of which Attenborough church was worth £16 and Annesley £5, indicating the importance of the acquisition of Attenborough. How many canons remained of this very poor house is not known. The prior was given a pension of only £6 which he lost almost immediately on acquiring the rectory of Attenborough.

Later History

After its dissolution in 1536 the priory passed through several hands, and nothing is known of the destruction of the monastic buildings and its early transformation into a domestic dwelling. During the Civil War it was used as a garrison by Royalist troops and then ransacked. The Parliamentarian and regicide Geoffrey Millington, whose family had owned Felley since 1603, was well compensated for this by Parliament in 1652. There is still evidence of sixteenth and seventeenth century building, and ten fireplaces in the older part, as given in the 1674 Hearth Tax return, can still be counted. It was to this earlier building that the late nineteenth-century additions were made.

The priory appears on the rentals of Mary Ann Chaworth of Annesley Hall at the end of the eighteenth century and finally came into the possession of John Musters of Colwick Hall, whom she married in 1805. Mary Ann was descended from Patricius Chaworth who had come over at the Conquest. It was a descendant of his who had married into the Annesley family in 1440. The house remains in the Chaworth Musters family to this day. The garden, re-landscaped in the past twenty years after earlier work, is open to the public as part of the National Gardens Scheme.

The Norman font at Annesley church

Access
OS SK 486 513. Half a mile on the A608 going west from M1 Junction 27. The house is not open to the public. The garden is currently open; please check for dates and times.

Newstead Priory

David Bewley

The Priory of St Mary of Newstead in Sherwood was formally founded as a house of Augustinian canons in about 1170 by Henry II. However, since there were royal grants to the 'canons of Sherwood' in 1163-64, its existence may well pre-date its foundation charter. The foundation endowment included not only Kighill and Ravenshead, but also the township of Papplewick with its church and mill, the waterside meadow of Bestwood and 100s of rents. Gifts of lands in Nottinghamshire by two other donors were also confirmed.

The priory's rather remote situation, a mile to the west of the present main road from Nottingham to Mansfield, is deceptive. Until the mid-eighteenth century the highway, which still exists as a footpath, ran close to the priory itself, which in medieval times lay at the edge of the royal Forest of Sherwood. Even today the ponds and stream, the ling and bracken-covered moorlands remind us that a major part of the original endowment was the carefully delineated forest wastes of Kighill and Ravenshead - names which are familiar still.

Architectural History

The first building to be erected was a small church, constructed from its eastern end beginning with the high altar and choir, and then the nave, but no side aisles. The domestic buildings were added gradually. There were probably never more than a dozen canons. Then, in the late thirteenth century, the Norman church was replaced by a larger church with transepts, side chapels and a north aisle. No south aisle was added, presumably to avoid considerable consequent rebuilding. The new church was started at its east end, with construction moving westwards down the new north aisle to the present west front, then turning back along the south to join the existing south wall, where there is a difference in foundation levels. The floor level of the church was probably a foot below the present ground level. Excavations show that a wall ran from north to south on the church site (opposite the second buttress from the west), and this may well have been the west wall of the first church. Although the memorial to Boatswain, Byron's dog, was supposedly erected on the site of the high altar, more probably it marks the eastern end wall of the church, with the high altar situated to the west of it.

The extensive alterations and additions by the Byrons after the Dissolution and by Colonel Wildman in the nineteenth century have destroyed or masked the greater part of the medieval monastic buildings. But remnants of the original twelfth century buildings remain in the form of a doorway into the south cloister, another (heavily restored) out of the north cloister, and in a blocked east processional doorway from the north cloister into the choir of the church. The extensive thirteenth century rebuilding is evidenced not only by the rebuilt church but by the undercroft, the slype (formerly a passage from the east cloister) and the 'Dark Entry' (a passage from the south cloister), there are also remains of the day stairs from the canons' dormitory to the south cloister, and a blocked thirteenth century doorway from the west cloister. The fourteenth and fifteenth centuries saw the rebuilding of the cloister walks - single-storey with sloping roofs - and of the Prior's Hall (now the much-altered Great Hall) and Prior's Parlour. It is likely that this was done to provide the priory with a set of rooms in keeping with the status of the important visitors who stayed at Newstead.

Economic History

New donations added to the original endowment. In the early thirteenth century Robert de Lexington gave the priory all the land of Scarcliffe, with the townships of Staythorpe and Rowthorn in Derbyshire. John de Stutevill had similarly given 40s rent and a quarter of wheat annually out of the manor of Kirkby-in-Ashfield. There were also further royal gifts, but the total of these new grants was not very considerable. In 1291 the priory's taxable income of £86 13s 6d placed it only halfway in the financial ranking order of Nottinghamshire monasteries. Moreover, Newstead had been, and continued, in deep financial trouble. As early as 1229 Stapleford church had been appropriated to the priory, with the permission of Archbishop Gray of York, because of the priory's poverty. In 1274 it was so seriously in debt that Robert de Sutton was appointed to take custody of it during the king's pleasure, and five years later permission was given to fell and sell the timber of a 40 acre wood given 34 years earlier.

Both the king and the Archbishop of York were involved in attempts to restore Newstead to financial health. In 1295, at the request of the prior and canons, the king appointed Hugh de Vienna to take charge of their revenues and, after reasonable sustenance for the prior, canons and their men, to use the remainder to relieve debts. During his custody no sheriff or bailiff was allowed to lodge on the premises. Peter de Leicester, the king's clerk, followed as custodian in 1300, and then John de Hothun. But at his Visitation in 1302 Archbishop Corbridge found misconduct and financial chaos, and appointed a special commission to manage Newstead's finances. In 1330 the Crown remitted £4 rents due for land at Linby because of the priory's poverty. A prime reason for these problems was set out by the Archbishop of York in 1320:

> The same priory, which is situated in a wood near the public road, is, by reason of the distances of the villages on every side, so grievously and continually burthened beyond the resources of its possessions, which are notoriously slender and scanty, by hospitality both to rich and poor, that the very things which are in readiness for its daily victuals have to be made common and set before guests who come unexpectedly to the priory.[1]

Those guests frequently included royalty, not surprisingly in view of the priory's situation in a royal forest used for hunting, and on a main highway to the north. King John stayed in 1201, Edward I in 1280, 1290 and 1300, and Edward II in 1307 and 1315, and the newly-crowned Edward III in 1327. The unavoidable expenditure these visits entailed may have been partly offset by the gifts received during them. On the other hand, it was in this period that major building and rebuilding was taking place, no doubt contributing to the priory's money problems, as did the evidence of gross misconduct noted below.

By 1535 the priory's taxable income had increased considerably from its 1291 level to a gross amount of £220, but deductions, including payments to the sister house at Thurgarton, daily expenditure on food and drink for the poor, and Maundy money, reduced income to a total of £168. The increase arose almost entirely from temporalities, and of this the major part related to income from demesne funds. The priory was also successful in increasing its income from its early endowments such as Papplewick and Hucknall Torkard. Perhaps its financial difficulties had stimulated the prior and canons into making greater efforts to increase the returns from their existing resources. Newstead, however, continued to rank amongst the middle-income monasteries of Nottinghamshire.

Whilst Newstead's income from spiritualities was comparatively small, certain endowments had involved obligations for the canons. In 1334 William de Cossall was licensed to alienate property in Cossall and Nottingham to the priory in order to provide three chaplains to celebrate mass daily for his soul and the souls of his ancestors and descendants. In 1341 Henry, William and Robert de Edwinstowe were licensed to alienate lands to provide two chaplains to celebrate mass daily in St Mary's church, Edwinstowe. The priory undertook to pay one of these chaplains ten marks a year for stipends for himself and the other chaplains, and a further mark for Henry's *obit*.

Monastic Life

The prior and canons were subject to Visitations not only by the Provincial Visitors of the Augustinian Order but also by the Archbishop of York, in whose diocese the priory lay. In 1252 Archbishop Gray found the prior and canons 'in hearty observance of their rules and lovers of peace and concord'. However, he ordered the prior, sub-prior and three or four older canons to audit the cellarer's accounts at least annually, and to take an inventory of all rents, the assizes of bread and ale and all stocks. In addition, intrusion to the cloister, refectory and other quiet places by boys and disorderly persons was to be prevented.

Seven years later further injunctions were added. The prior was exhorted to do his best to obtain grace and favour with patrons by personally receiving guests with a smiling

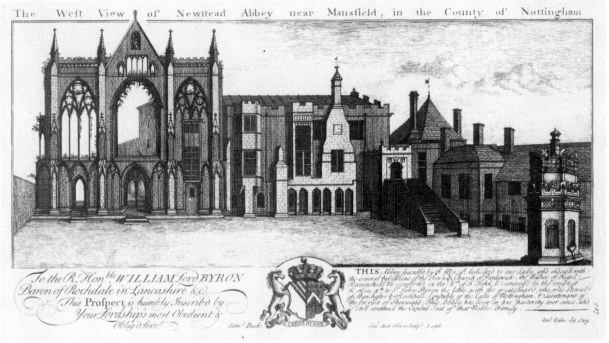

Samuel Buck's engraving of the west view of Newstead Abbey, 1726

countenance. He was to merit the love of the priory by doing nothing without consultation with the older canons. There was to be no drinking or wandering outside the cloister after Compline. These instructions suggest managerial shortcomings at this time rather than major spiritual failings. Further evidence of this is provided by the findings of the Provincial Visitors of the Order, the Priors of Nostell and Guisborough, who visited Newstead two years later, and drew up regulations for the control of the monastery's affairs. Certain canons were chosen to receive all the income of the priory and to distribute it to the cellarer and other obedientiaries, as necessary. A requirement was set out for accounts to be presented by all recipients, not only by the cellarer and chamberlain, twice a year (or at least once). Again, the lack of proper management and financial control is evident.

More serious trouble followed. In 1280 Archbishop Wickwane punished two canons for the benefit of their morals and dismissed two others, Roger of the Cellar and Geoffery of the Kitchen, as a 'nuisance to the monastery'. He also ordered that canons' lockers were to be inspected

to prevent the harbouring of private property and, again, persons of low condition and strangers were not to enter the infirmary or wander the cloisters.

There is a suggestion here, perhaps, of corruption and good living. In 1293 Archbishop Romeyn utterly forbade the game of dice and removed the sacrist from his office for insolence and for misappropriating a loan. In 1307 the prior himself was accused of incontinence with one woman and of relapsing into incontinence with another. The prior contested the allegations, but in January 1308 a commissioner was appointed to receive his purgation. Six years later, the sub-prior was deprived of his office because he had 'abused it to the damage of the house'. He was placed on a restricted diet for a year and instructed to say a penitential psalm and litany, prostrate before the altar, every Friday. That the priory was also in great financial trouble at this time, as mentioned above, is no surprise in the light of this evidence.

The resignation of Prior Richard de Grange in 1324 is evidence that the priory's relationship with the Crown and its religious superiors could cause problems. Two canons took the news to the king, who was at Nottingham, and they were given his leave to elect a new prior. One of the canons of Newstead, William de Thurgarton, was elected with the king's approval, but the Archbishop of York, when informed of this, quashed the election on the grounds that the right of preferment lay with him. Having thus asserted his claim, he too chose William de Thurgarton!

An unusual sidelight on the multifarious functions of medieval monasteries and their residents is shown in 1355 when the Sheriff of Nottingham was ordered to send the tools of Edmund of St Andrew, a canon of Newstead, from the priory to Westminster, where Edmund was employed as master of the works in St Stephen's chapel. It is interesting to speculate whether Edmund had been similarly engaged at Newstead. A puzzling incident was the royal command of 8 May 1238 that the prior and canons should pass to Thomas de Dunholmia, citizen of London, all the goods of the late Joan, Queen of Scots, deposited with the priory after her death by Brother John de Sancto Egidio and Henry Balliol. Why they were deposited at Newstead is not clear, but the incident is an example of the use of the priory as a safe deposit for valuables.

The Dissolution

The last prior, John Blake, was appointed in September 1526. When the smaller monasteries were dissolved a decade later, Newstead, with a net income below the £200 threshold, sought to avert dissolution by payment of a fine of £233 - more than its annual income. But its license to continue did not avail it long; on 21 July 1539 it was surrendered to the Crown Commissioners. Presumably it was at this time that the canons hid their bronze eagle lectern and two candlesticks in the square pond to the east of the priory, now known as the Eagle Pond. There they remained until their discovery in the late eighteenth century. Bought by Sir Richard Kaye from the fifth Lord Byron in 1775, the lectern was presented to Southwell Minster in 1805, where it remains. The canons were treated quite generously at the Dissolution, the prior being granted a pension of £26 13s 4d, the sub-prior one of £6 and ten canons amounts ranging from £3 6s 8d to £5 6s 8d.

The eagle lectern at Southwell Minster

Later History

In May 1540 a courtier, Sir John Byron of Colwick, paid £810 for the priory and its possessions. The fabric was not apparently in a good state, for Leland, riding by it at about this time wrote, 'A little or I came to the edge of this wood, I left about a quarter of a mile on the right hand the ruins of Newstead, a priory of canons'.[2] Byron renamed the priory 'Newstead Abbey' and began transforming it into a house appropriate to his status. He first demolished the church, apart from the great west façade. Over the ensuing years the Byrons made Newstead their sole home, disposing of their other estates. They made the refectory into a drawing room, built galleries over the cloisters, and subdivided the dormitory into bedrooms.

In 1644 Newstead was pillaged by the Roundheads, the Byron brothers being fervent Royalists. The eldest, Sir John, was raised by Charles I to the peerage in 1643 as Baron Byron of Rochdale. After the Civil War the second Lord Byron, Richard, did much to restore and improve the Abbey and the estate. But the final decades of the eighteenth century brought increasing financial problems. The fine picture collection was sold, the estate timber cut down and by 1798 when George Gordon, the most famous Lord Byron, inherited Newstead at the age of ten, the Abbey was in a deplorable state. The Great Hall was empty except for a quantity of hay and Byron used it for pistol practice. But he fell in love with Newstead, though he spent comparatively little time there. He could afford to furnish only the Prior's Parlour and a couple of rooms above it. His huge debts forced him to put the estate up for sale in 1812. It was not until 1817 that his old school friend, Colonel Thomas Wildman, bought it for £94,500.

Colonel Wildman spent his family fortune on Newstead and the appearance and substance of the Abbey today are largely his creation and that of his architect, John Shaw. Ownership passed to the Webb family in 1859 and then to Sir Julien Cahn in 1925, who presented it to Nottingham Corporation in 1931, which still owns it. It is perhaps appropriate that after eight centuries of vicissitudes, Newstead still affords the welcome and hospitality to the visitor which the Augustinian canons, much to their cost, gave for 370 years.

References

1. H.F. Wagstaff, *Handbook and Guide to Newstead Abbey* (Hucknall, 1931), 7-8

2. V.W. Walker (revised M.J. Howell), *The House of Byron* (1988), 27

Access

OS SK 540 538. Newstead Abbey (as the Priory is now known) lies some 12 miles north of Nottingham off the main A60 road from Nottingham to Mansfield. Regular bus services from Nottingham to Mansfield stop at the lodge gates and there is a special summer service from Nottingham to the Abbey. There is a car park and restaurant. Opening times for the Abbey and the grounds vary. Please contact for details.

Mattersey Priory

Jean Nicholson

Founded in 1185 by Roger, son of Ranulph de Mattersey, the priory of Mattersey in the wapentake of Bassetlaw was one of the few Gilbertine monasteries to be established outside of Lincolnshire. It never appears to have been one of the 'double houses' for which the Gilbertines were famous and records and archaeological remains suggest that only male canons were ever present. The priory was dedicated to St Helen, and a cast of the conventual seal in the British Museum shows what appears to be St Helen adoring the cross. Situated about a mile east of the village of Mattersey, the priory was built on a slight rise in the carrland near the river Idle. The road from Mattersey to Wiseton probably passed close to the priory, making it less isolated than it appears today. Since it was also close to the Roman road leading to the crossing of the river Trent at Littleborough, contact with Lincoln and the Gilbertine monasteries of Lincolnshire would have been relatively easy.

Architectural History

Few remains of the priory are visible above ground, but excavations during the 1930s established the position of the main buildings, and their outline can be clearly seen today. The arcading of the cloister and the arches of the refectory undercroft confirm a thirteenth century date for most of the buildings. All that remains of the church is part of a tower wall and a long narrow nave. No identifiable artefacts have been found on the site, but when the floor of Mattersey church was relaid in the eighteenth century, two carved panels were found buried under the chancel pavement. Showing St Helen and St Martin, their style closely resembles work found elsewhere in Lincolnshire and Nottinghamshire. A date of about 1325 has been suggested and it is possible that they were part of a reredos in the

priory church. More remains may lie under the garden of the adjoining farmhouse, the east wall of which shows similarities to the remains of the church tower. Dowsing showed that it may have been part of a gatehouse. It is recorded that the priory suffered a disastrous fire in 1279 and the walls of the church show evidence of having been burnt. Very little building appears to have taken place after this traumatic event.

Fragment of some of the remaining wall structure

Before the fire the priory appears to have been flourishing, with the prior making his presence felt in the area. The Hundred Rolls of 1275 record that the Prior of Mattersey was charged with encroaching on to the road leading from Mattersey to Gringley-on-the-Hill, so that it was scarcely possible for a cart to make its way there. In 1276 the prior claimed privileges of freedom from pontage, passage and any kind of toll or customs and from hundred and other dues throughout England and free warren in his demesne lands of Mattersey and Thorpe. In support of these claims he produced a charter of Henry III dated 1251.

Following the fire, on 20 November 1279, Archbishop Wickwane of York ordered an inquisition regarding the alleged destruction of the charters and muniments. On 5 December a certificate from the office of the Archdeacon of Nottingham stated that a jury had declared that Mattersey had possessed a document under the seal of Archbishop Gray assigning to them an annual pension of five marks out of the churches of Misson and Gamston-on-Idle. In October 1280 a diocesan licence for the appropriation of Mattersey church to the priory was obtained 'in consequence of their poverty through fire'. The priory was exempted from paying tithes on the priory fisheries, tannery or mills to the vicar of the church. It was also exempt from paying the tithes on gardens and orchards at 'Bachow' grange (possibly connected with the present Blaco Hill).

Economic History

The *Taxatio* of Pope Nicholas in 1291 gives the total annual income as £52, one of the lowest for Nottinghamshire religious houses. But at the beginning of the fourteenth century attempts were made to rebuild and regain some of the priory's wealth and standing. At the end of the reign of Edward I, Isabel de Chauncey gave the priory all lands and tenements it had by gift of her ancestor in Bassetlaw and Lancashire, also the advowsons of the churches of Mattersey, Gamston, Misson and Bolton. In 1403 Henry IV granted the priory a weekly market on Monday at Mattersey and two annual fairs, one on the vigil and day of St John of Beverley and the other on the vigil and day of St Simon and St Jude. But Mattersey never recovered from the 'severe fire' which 'wrought dire destruction'. Archaeological evidence suggests that the church and monastic buildings were never fully rebuilt.

No documents from Mattersey Priory appear to have survived, all Gilbertine documents kept at Sempringham being destroyed by fire in the seventeenth century. The priory gets scant mention in ecclesiastical and official documents. What records there are give a tantalising glimpse of a small community trying to serve God and eke out a living on a tiny income in an unfavourable environment.

The latter half of the thirteenth century marked the beginning of the 'Little Ice Age'. In the early years of the fourteenth century climatic changes led to poor harvests and murrain in sheep and cattle. In 1349 the Black Death was responsible for a dramatic drop in the population. Although the direct effect on Mattersey is not known, nearly a third of the beneficed clergy in the deanery of Retford were replaced between March 1349 to March 1350, suggesting that the Black Death was rampant in north Nottinghamshire. These events must have affected not only the ability and will to rebuild, but also the amount of money available in rents and endowments with which to do so. The *Valor Ecclesiasticus* of 1535 gives the net income of Mattersey as £55. Unlike most Nottinghamshire monasteries it had failed to increase its income.

Monastic Life

The number of canons and lay brothers was not sufficient to farm the priory land directly, and much was rented out. In the Inquisition Post Mortem of Peter Pole of October 1514 mention is made of land in Mattersey held of the Prior and Convent of Mattersey by service worth 43s 4d yearly. One of the few indications that the priory was involved in village life was a reference to Prior Thomas Sutton acting as godfather to Thomas Wentworth, son of Matthew Wentworth of Everton, in 1487. However, such a small religious community, which possessed a water mill, windmill and fishery, could hardly have led a life apart from the village. It is possible that many of the canons were from local families.

The Dissolution

At the Visitation of Layton and Legh in 1536 'one incontinent sought release'. On October 1538 Mattersey was surrendered by Robert Holgate, Bishop of Llandaff and Commendatory Grand Master of the Order of Sempringham. At the Dissolution there were a prior and four canons. The prior, Thomas Norman, does not appear to have fared badly. He received a pension of £12, and later became headmaster of Malton Grammar School in Yorkshire, founded by Robert Holgate in 1546. The sub-prior, Thomas Bell, received a pension of £2 13s 4d. He may have quickly married; for later in 1538 a Thomas Bell

Remains of the refectory showing thirteenth century arcading

married Jennit Pasoke at Mattersey. The remaining three canons, John Garton, William Schylton and Richard Watson, received pensions of £2 each.

Later History

The site with all the buildings, together with the manor of Mattersey, was granted to Anthony Nevill and his wife Mary. Anthony was the son of Alexander Nevill of South Leverton and was also related to Sir John Hercy, who was working for Cromwell. The Nevills took up residence at Mattersey, and took their responsibilities as lords of the manor seriously. Much of the land remained in the family until the late nineteenth century, when the estate was owned by the Rev. Christopher Nevill.

<table>
<tr><td>Access</td></tr>
<tr><td>OS SK703895. An English Heritage managed site with ruins of church, cloisters and refectory. Almost one mile along farm track from Mattersey church off B6045, six miles northeast of East Retford. Signposted from main road. Car park at site: open dawn till dusk.</td></tr>
</table>

Beauvale Charterhouse

Marie Wilkinson

St Bruno, born in Cologne around 1030, founded La Grande Chartreuse on a remote mountain side in the Alps in 1084. But it was Guigo, elected prior in 1090, who established the monastery as the headquarters of a new Order. He wrote the 'customs' in 1128 and attracted many adherents. The first English Charterhouse was founded on a royal vill at Witham in Somerset in 1178, probably as part of Henry II's penance for the murder of Archbishop Thomas Becket. Thereafter, however, the Order was slow to expand in England. This may have been due to their hermit lifestyle as well as their refusal to eat meat, even when ill, at a time when meat was considered especially important for health.

Whatever the reason, Beauvale was only the third English Charterhouse when it was founded by Sir Nicholas de Cantilupe, Lord of Ilkeston, in 1343. Not only this: it was the first Nottinghamshire monastery of any Order to be established for 150 years (apart from houses of friars) and the last to be established in the county (with the exception of the Newark Observants). Nicholas had been knighted for military services to the Crown and saw action at the battle of Crecy. His motives in founding the new house are not known; but he was much influenced by Prior Thomas of Hinton, under whose auspices the second English Charterhouse, was founded. In October Nicholas bound himself to Thomas in the sum of £1000 to be paid at Greasley on the Feast of All Saints, if within three years he had not built at his own cost a church and house for a prior and twelve monks. The wording of this indenture suggests that building had in fact already begun, as the foundation charters drawn up a few weeks later confirm. The site was Nicholas' park at Greasley and was by no means remote; no doubt this helped the rapid establishment of the monastery.

On 9 December, royal permission having been received, two foundation charters were signed. The first, witnessed by the Archbishop of York and other senior clerics and nobles, declared that Nicholas had given 'to the prior and monks of the Carthusian Order in the monastery, which is called Beautiful Vale (*Pulchra Vallis* in the original Latin) built for their use, the said monastery and park adjacent' together with land and rent in the vills of Greasley and Selston and the advowsons of the churches there. The endowment was more precisely described in the second charter and included 300 acres, ten messuages and twelve bovates in Greasley, and thirteen messuages and seventeen bovates in Selston. Four years later Nicholas made a further substantial donation, which included all his demesne in Selston and seventeen villeins and their land in Greasley. Finally, just before his death in 1354, he added the church of Farnham, Yorkshire in the diocese of York.

Architectural History

Excavation has shown the priory, though small, had a typical set of Carthusian monastic buildings, including a church, prior's house and the monks' cells and gardens built around the larger of two cloisters. It was built of dark red sandstone with dressings to the doors and windows of Derbyshire gritstone. The second charter refers to the monks' 'churches and houses', suggesting Beauvale was a primitive Carthusian type with separate sets of buildings for the monks on the one hand and the lay-brothers and *redditi* on the other, but this is not supported by excavation evidence.

The church was the first building to be erected. Like other Carthusian churches, it was a plain structure without aisles or arcades. There were two entrances for the two choirs, the western one for the lay brethren and the eastern for the monks. The buildings were in a rectangular area 470ft x 290ft, the western half of which was taken up by the cloister and its surrounding cells and gardens. The gatehouse lay in the south-east corner of the site, with a room of about 20ft square on either side. There were, in total, fourteen cells arranged around three sides of the great cloister, each being a well-built structure of two storeys. The ground floor was divided into four small rooms: a lobby, a living-room with a door to the garden, a bedroom and a study. The upper floor was probably a single large workroom. Outside a pentise led to a wooden garderobe over a stream, which ran past the outer wall of the monastery.

The decaying remains of the prior's house

There is little evidence of rebuilding, but in 1370 John of Gaunt granted the priory the manor of Etwall in Derbyshire worth £12 *per annum* for the repair of the priory. At the end of the fifteenth century the prior's cell, which was three storeys high, was rebuilt. A circular staircase was introduced, giving access to the upper floors, which each housed a comfortable room warmed by a fireplace and lit by windows overlooking the great cloister.

Economic History

In spite of Nicholas de Cantilupe's considerable generosity, the priory was felt to be poorly endowed. Within a few years William de Aldeburgh had given it some waste land adjoining its property, 'considering how moderately they were endowed, particularly as to pastures for their animals, without which, it seemed to him, they could not be sustained'. In 1293 William's two daughters granted a manor for the founding of a chantry, whereby two monks were to pray exclusively for the family. This probably increased the number of monks to fourteen. The priory also benefited from royal patronage. Edward III gave a tonne of Gascon wine annually; his daughter Isabella an annual pension of 100s; and John of Gaunt the manor of Etwell. The priory's difficulties extended into the next century. In 1403 the king gave Beauvale the Lincolnshire property of St Fromond's Priory in Normandy, taken over as a result of

the French wars. But ten years later the monks had to sell some of this because they had no money or goods to sell to buy stock for their lands, 'pay their debts or relieve their necessity'. The reasons for the priory's problems are not clear. In 1535 Beauvale's net taxable income was assessed at £196, higher than either Newstead or Rufford. Moreover, it had the benefit of coal on its land probably from the start. Certainly in 1397 the priory leased a coal mine in Kirkestallaund to William Monyasche and others for a weekly rent of 4s 6d per pit. This was halved if water or 'dampe' prevented them from working more than two and a half days a week if they got any coal.

For their part the monks obtained a 99-year lease for 13s 4d annually of the right to all the coal in Selston parish, together with the wood growing there, for making 'punches and props'. It is possible they exploited this directly through their own workforce. They also seem to have sold coal commercially; for the *Valor* notes payments to Sir John Chaworth and others for the movement of coal out of the area. The priory also benefited from ironmaking on its lands. Shortly before the Dissolution, it received £10 for a 'house called the Smethey in Greasley with an inclosure for making iron, for which he should have paid £12 17s 8d but that he found not stones to make the iron'.

Monastic Life

The Carthusians were the strictest of all the orders established in England, and the first to die for their faith when the Reformation came. The enclosed nature of life at Beauvale meant that in the worldly sense it had little history; certainly little of what happened was recorded. Each monk had his own cell or set of rooms where he spent his time. Apart from the official 'Provincials' on their tours of inspection, there were few visitors. Very occasionally a monk was transferred between Charterhouses, as in 1429 when Dom John Joliis was sent in custody from Beauvale to the monastery of the Holy Spirit at Gosnay. Even the poor collecting their alms of bread were not allowed into the priory but were dealt with at the porter's lodge.

The Carthusian Order was ruled by its General Chapter which met annually. All priors were expected to attend, but because of the distance the English priors were required only to send representatives every leap year. But even this occasional contact was sometimes lacking. The problems this caused were exacerbated by the failure of letters to get through. A missive sent to England in 1429 stated that:

> Whereas the priors of Witham, Beauvale, London and Bethleem (Sheen) have written complaining ... that their writings ... are not answered ... , the General Chapter replies that, saving their peace, it answered as often as they wrote; if answers did not reach them, it was not the fault of the Chapter, but their own, for not sending a proper messenger and for not coming to the Chapter as they are bound to do.[1]

There were probably faults on both sides, for there is evidence the General Chapter did not always reply quickly. Moreover, correspondence which did get through reveals a continuing failure to keep the English houses fully informed. For example, it was only in 1470 that the English discovered they were allowed to have a fire in the refectory in winter, and not until the sixteenth century that only gloves of white cloth could be worn when riding in bad weather. Differences in culture also hindered understanding. In 1356 the English did not know the meaning of several words in the statutes, including *cellaria* (places where wine was stored near the vineyards) and *birettus* (what prelates and doctors wore on their heads).

Normally the Visitors to the English houses were themselves English. In 1427 the Prior of Beauvale in his capacity of chief Visitor travelled to Witham, Lincolnshire to confirm the election of a new prior following the resignation of the previous one. Twenty years later and again in 1463 Beauvale's prior was once more a Visitor. These instances survive from the very scant records still extant, suggesting that, in spite of its small size and fairly remote situation, Beauvale played a full role in Carthusian affairs. Moreover, the absence of any serious disciplinary or financial scandals at Beauvale indicate that life there was peaceful and the attainment of Carthusian ideals the norm.

The Dissolution

Robert Lawrence had been Prior of Beauvale for four years when he set out to the London Charterhouse in 1535 to see his predecessor at Beauvale, Prior John Houghton. His

reasons for doing this are not known for certain, but they must have been many in those troubled times. Two days after his arrival he was joined by Augustine Webster, Prior of Axholme, and Houghton decided they should visit Thomas Cromwell, a decision that eventually resulted in their deaths.

John Houghton begged leave to ask three questions of Cromwell, part of the first one being 'How could the king, a layman, be head of the Church of England?'. No other questions were allowed, a charge of treason and arrest being Cromwell's answer. They were kept in the Tower for some days before being taken to Cromwell's residence called the 'Rolls'. There on 20 April 1535, in the presence of Cromwell, Edward Foxe, the King's Almoner, John Bell and John Tregunwell, Doctors in Law, Thomas Bedyll, Archdeacon of Cornwall, Richard Rich, the King's Solicitor, and Ralph Sadler, questions were put to Lawrence and Webster. Some days later all three Carthusians and Richard Reynolds, a Brigettine priest, were visited by Cromwell and the royal commissioners. With them they brought a copy of the Supremacy Act. Questions asked by Cromwell were answered, and the answers can still be found in documents in the Public Record Office in London. Robert Lawrence stated 'That there is one Catholic Church and one Divine, of which the Bishop of Rome is the head; therefore, he cannot believe that the King is supreme head of the Church'.[2] The others replied likewise.

On Thursday 29 April 1535, the trial of the Carthusians for treason took place at Westminster Hall. Finding them guilty was not easy, however. The jury would not condemn them, and Cromwell sent a message stating 'That if you do not find them guilty you yourselves shall die the traitor's death'. It was not until he finally went in person to the jury with more threats that the accused were found guilty as charged.

On 4 May 1535, Robert Lawrence, John Houghton, Augustine Webster, Richard Reynolds and John Haile, were taken from the Tower to Tyburn. They were to lie down upon hurdles to be drawn to Tyburn. The night before rain had fallen, and the sight of monks in their religious habits, splashed by rain, was not one seen before by the people assembled along the way. The rough stones that made up the road and the dirt from the rain soaking their white habits made a painful sight, but the nature of their death was to be even more painful. Sir Thomas More saw them leave the Tower and later wrote 'They went to their death as bridegrooms to their marriage'.[3]

The gallows consisted of upright poles with a beam across the top. A cauldron stood nearby. The priests were taken from the hurdles, John Houghton being the first to be executed. He spoke to the awaiting crowds:

> I call upon the Lord of Heaven and earth, and I beseech you all beloved, in the dread day of judgement to testify with me, that here, about to die, I publicly declare that I refuse to comply with the wishes of our lord the King, not out of any pertinacity, malice or rebellious spirit, but solely through the fear of God.[4]

He then prayed. He was hanged but cut down while still alive. His entrails were then cut from him and thrown into the prepared fire. Finally, his still beating heart was torn from his body. After his death one arm was cut off and nailed over the gateway of the London Charterhouse. Robert Lawrence of Beauvale was the second priest to go to the gallows. He and the others suffered the same cruel death as John Houghton. They were the first martyrs of the Reformation and Tyburn became the place where over 100 more met their deaths during the Reformation.

Beauvale had lost its prior but the Charterhouse was still alive if only for a short time. The last prior, Thomas Woodcock, appointed in December 1537, surrendered, so we are told, dressed in a short gown and velvet cap, to Dr London, Cromwell's agent. He received an annual pension of £25 13s 4d. Eight monks received £5 6s 0d *per annum* and two lay brothers, described as 'converse and aged men', were given 40s. Nicholas Dugmer is the only monk of Beauvale who can be traced until his death. When asked to take the vow of supremacy, his reply was 'I take him (i.e. the king) as God and the Holy Church take him; and I am sure he taketh himself no otherwise'.[5] His answer was accepted. When Beauvale was surrendered, he made his way eventually to another house at Louvain, but only after much travelling to and from England. He died at Louvain in the Low Countries on 10 September 1578, having been in the Carthusian Order for 50 years.

Later History

After some years in the king's hands Beauvale was given to Sir William Hussey of London, but soon passed to the Morrison family. One of their heirs, Charles White, saw his sister Bridget married in 1604 from the farmhouse adjoining the ruins of the priory. From them Beauvale passed to the Capels, Earls of Essex. The area now belongs to the Barber family who for many years have enjoyed both the land and the local coal mines once owned by the monks. The priory remains are in bad condition and some of them appear to be in danger of imminent collapse. A pilgrimage is held once a year on the site of the priory, on the nearest Sunday to 4 May, the date of the death of Prior Robert Lawrence. Mass is still celebrated and Robert Lawrence and John Houghton still remembered. St Robert Lawrence was beatified in 1886 and canonised as one of the Forty Martyrs of England and Wales in 1970.

References

1. E.M. Thompson, *The Carthusian Order in England* (SPCK London, 1930), 300-1

2. *Ibid.*, p.394

3. L. Hendricks, *The London Charterhouse: Its Monks and its Martyrs* (London, 1889), 150-2

4. *Cause of the Canonisation of Blessed Martyrs John Houghton, Robert Lawrence, Augustine Webster, Richard Reynolds, et al.* (Sacred Congregation of Rites, Vatican Polyglot Press, 1968), 38

5. L. Hendricks, *The London Charterhouse*, 303-5

Access

OS 493490. The site is on private property and access can be gained only by permission from the farmer in residence. The site is reached along a minor road off B600 at Moorgreen, near Eastwood.

The Military Orders

Barry Alexander

The Knights Hospitallers established a commandery at Ossington through the gift of Roger de Buron. But his father Hugh had already given the church there to Lenton Priory in 1144 and had become a Cluniac monk 'that God might avert the scourge of his wrath from him, due to the very great multitude of sins'. This caused lengthy litigation with Lenton before the Hospitallers finally obtained the right of presentation of the church of Ossington. Nearby Winkburn, originally donated to the commandery at Newland, Yorkshire, became a *camera* of Ossington.

The other military order, the Knights Templars, had little property in Nottinghamshire. The Close Rolls of 1213, record a house in St Mary's parish, Nottingham, as 'their free hospice', a provision for travelling knights. An Inquisition Post Mortem in 1275 shows them holding land at Coddington and Thorpe near Newark, and rents from Newark. The advowson of Sibthorpe church was theirs too. The Templars, from vows of poverty and asceticism, came to have immense wealth and international power. Attacked and pillaged by Philip IV of France, the French Pope Clement V had to dissolve the Order in 1312. Most of their properties were transferred to the Knights Hospitallers.

In 1338, Prior Philip de Thame made a detailed return of the Hospitallers' English possessions to the Grand Master. The total receipts and expenses of the 'Bajulia de Oscington' were £95 and £77 respectively and for the *camera* at Winkburn £62 and £22. The higher labour and administrative costs at Ossington are evident. These returns included the chapel at Maplebeck, Winkburn church and messuages at Danethorpe and Thurmeton, but rents at Sibthorpe were paid to the commandery at Eagle, in Lincolnshire. Ossington had two windmills; 60 quarters of grain, value £9, were required each year for the bakehouse there. At Winkburn, 20 quarters were used from their windmill. Wool, a valuable export in Edward III's reign, influenced the number of sheep kept. At Ossington, 600 sheep were pastured for others and at Winkburn 500, all at 1d a head. However, no income from the sale of wool is shown.

From this return the distribution of commanderies in adjacent counties is found. Derbyshire had only one at Yeaveley, plus a camera at Barrow-on-Trent. In Leicestershire there were five sites in total, but two were *camerae*; in south Yorkshire there were only two commanderies. The main holding of the Hospitallers in the East Midlands, however, was in Lincolnshire with two commanderies and three former Templar houses. The average total income of these houses, including Ossington and its *camera*, was £132, ranging from £56 *per annum* at Newland, Yorkshire, to £284 *per annum* at Willoughton, Lincolnshire. This compares with an average of £112 and a range of £16 - 340 for the incomes of Nottinghamshire's twelve monasteries in 1291 (see Chapter 2). Though dated nearly 50 years apart, it can be shown that the two sets of data are similar. The income of the Hospitallers was thus almost as varied as that of the monasteries in this area.

At the Dissolution the gross value of Ossington and Winkburn was only £46, a considerable decline. By then it was recorded under the Yorkshire commandery of Newland, whose gross income had risen to £202. On the other hand the *Valor Ecclesiasticus* shows the gross income for Yeavely and Barrow, Derbyshire, had increased significantly to £267, similar in value to the commanderies in Leicestershire, now centralised under Rothley, which returned a gross income of £275. Much of the net income was paid away as responsions.

In 1540 the Hospitallers were suppressed and by 1542 'Ossington, a parcel of the late preceptory of Newland', together with Maltby, Temple Bruer, Eagle and others, was sold to Charles, Duke of Suffolk. Yeavely and Rothley followed the next year. Winkburn came into the possession of William Burnell, Auditor to Henry VIII. The family remained lords of the manor for nine generations, when the male line ended with the death of Darcy Burnell in 1774,

The church of St John of Jerusalem at Winkburn

though the property continues in the family to this day. In 1782 the old church at Ossington was rebuilt with the loss of one more link with the Hospitallers. Only in Winkburn does the church dedicated to St John of Jerusalem, one of only three in Britain, retain links with this Order. The headquarters of the Order remained in Malta until 1798. It then became a charitable institution at Rome. The present British Order of St John of Jerusalem, a secular institution, was given a royal charter in 1888. It carries out Red Cross and hospital duties.

Access

OS SK 712 584. Winkburn church and a Holy Well about a mile north-west of the village are all that remain to remind us of the preceptory and *camera* of the Knights Hospitallers in Nottinghamshire. Winkburn is about 3 miles north of Southwell off the A617.

The Hospitals of Nottinghamshire

Barbara Roper

The medieval Hospitals were a significant feature of the landscape, and nearly always fulfilled a dual function. Not only were they charitable institutions endowed for the care of the sick, the poor, the blind, the crippled and the old; they were also religious houses adhering to the monastic way of life. In the twelfth and thirteenth centuries many individuals sought to mitigate their time in purgatory, both for themselves and their loved ones, by the building and endowment of a house of religion. Sometimes this would be on a grand scale, but often a lesser establishment such as a hospital would suffice. In the original charter the donor included a dedication to a particular saint and stipulated the purpose of the endowment, frequently 'for the worship of God, and the sustenance of the sick poor and infirm'. The number of persons to be maintained was usually added, which was often small, perhaps two or three, and rarely exceeded thirteen. The saintly dedication was obviously the choice of the patron, but St Mary Magdalen was a favourite, as was St Leonard for the lazar houses.

In plan these hospitals comprised basically a church which doubled as an infirmary hall, certainly during the early medieval period. The centre aisle was left clear, while the beds were arranged down each side. This arrangement ensured that the bedridden could see the altar and partake of the Eucharist, which was considered to be a vital part of the healing process. A warden was in overall charge, a resident priest was engaged to conduct the daily offices, and sisters or brethren were required to nurse and care for the sick. Simple quarters in an annexe provided accommodation for the staff. Sometimes a meeting hall, or rooms for the able-bodied poor, were incorporated into the complex, possibly linked by a cloister.

In country districts accommodation for travellers or an inn were a further addition, as rural hospitals usually developed on pilgrim or other important routes. Consequently the extent of the buildings depended on a number of factors, including the generosity of the patron, the exact use to which they were being put, and the situation. More often than not the urban hospitals were a sanctuary for leprous persons, and thus marginalisation outside the town boundary was a necessity. Sometimes a hospital was purpose-built within the confines of a monastery; but, wherever the location, there had to be an association with water. This was a more subtle link than merely for drinking and washing, because water was also considered vital for spiritual cleansing. The medieval mind often connected illness with moral transgression, hence the importance of repentance and the washing away of sin as a therapeutic measure.

Of the thirteen hospitals documented in Nottinghamshire, six were lazar houses, the others for the sick poor and infirm. Some of the surviving references are scanty, some are detailed, not necessarily in proportion to the importance of the institution. Most probably the earliest foundations were in the towns of Nottingham and Newark.

Nottingham

Three twelfth century hospitals are recorded in Nottingham. The earliest was founded in the first half of the century, and although dedicated to St John the Baptist, may have originated as a secular institution. When in the mid-thirteenth century a substantial endowment was forthcoming from Robert de Fulk, the hospital was officially recognised by Pope Gregory IX and subsequently committed to the protection of the Archbishop of York. In 1241 a set of injunctions was issued from York and intimated that there were sisters as well as brethren in the hospital and both were to wear habits of russet and brown cloth. Their primary task was to tend to the necessities of the poor, but numerous regulations disciplined their daily lives and stipulated their religious observances.

For the next two centuries the hospital continued its valuable work, but then, as with so many other foundations, a gradual decline set in. Corruption started at the top, monies were misdirected, the assets dissipated and all charitable actions eventually abandoned. By 1538, when the monasteries and other religious houses were being dissolved, there was often very little left for confiscation by the Crown. A visiting antiquarian reported in 1540 'St John Hospital almost down'. The chapel and a barn, however, did survive on the site, alongside the main route north from Trent Bridge (now Glasshouse Street), and in 1627 these buildings were leased out 'to stand and be as a workhouse'. Thus St John's became in turn a workhouse, a house of correction, a prison, and a refuge for homeless women until it was finally demolished in 1900.

The second early house in Nottingham, the Hospital of the Holy Sepulchre, has always posed problems for local historians, whose conclusions have been largely based on supposition. Definite reference is made to a land gift by Robert de St Remy to the palmers (pilgrims) of Nottingham, enabling them to establish a hospital for poor men. This endowment was confirmed by a charter of Henry II in 1170. There were more references in the Patent Rolls a hundred years later, and in the Nottingham records of 1307 there is a locational directive; 'beyond the ditch of the town next to the cemetery of the Sepulchre'.

The third notable foundation in Nottingham was the leper hospital of St Leonard. Unfortunately there are no surviving records because in all probability they were lost in a disastrous fire which ravaged the complex in 1341. Alfred Stapleton, who did much research into these hospitals at the turn of the twentieth century, concluded that St Leonard's was annexed to the ancient church of St Michael and that the two buildings occupied the triangle of land to the north of Woodborough Road between Mansfield Road and Huntingdon Street. During the twelfth and thirteenth centuries it appeared to be a large self-sufficient establishment dependant upon charity and begging for alms.

Two other contrasting hospitals in the county town should be mentioned. One was an unpretentious lazar house outside the town ditch at West Bar (Chapel Bar). In 1330 Edward III, while staying in Nottingham, granted 'protection to the leprous men of the hospital of St Marry atte Westbarr, when collecting alms for the support of their house'. The

second began with a rich endowment donated by John Plumtree in 1390, to found a hospital in honour of the Annunciation of the Blessed Virgin. He did this for 'the good estate of the founder, his wife Emma, and for their souls after death and for the souls of their parents'. The hospital was built at Bridge End on the corner of Fisher Gate and was to house thirteen widows. Later due to a financial crisis the number was reduced to seven. After the Dissolution the hospital was confiscated by the Crown there then being no resident widows and the charitable revenue going solely to support two chantry priests. A hundred years later Huntingdon Plumtree rebuilt the hospital and once more it provided a home for thirteen widows. In 1823 another building was designed for the site and is still proudly standing, although the thirteen widows have long since gone. A fascinating historical synopsis is inscribed over the doorway, but sadly the building is empty and neglected and currently up for sale.

Mention must also be made of the hospital of St Anthony, incorporated in the great priory at Lenton. In all probability this would have fulfilled all the functions required of a medieval hospital; as a sanctuary for the old and dying, to sustain the poor and infirm, and to rest and restore the traveller. It had a special interest in the treatment of those suffering from 'St Anthony's fire' or erysipelas.

Newark

Bishop Alexander the Magnificent of Lincoln (1123-1148) was politically ambitious and a great builder of military strongholds, one of which was Newark Castle, but he also established many religious houses. In Newark he richly endowed 'a hospital house for the infirm poor of Christ', which he dedicated to St Leonard. This dedication, coupled with the site 'near Newark', actually on Northgate, suggests that the infirm poor may have been lepers. Various documents over the next two hundred years mention further endowments and gifts of land, a notable one in 1312 by William Durant:

To our beloved in Christ, the master of the Hospital of St Leonard in Newark for providing a chaplain to celebrate divine service every day in the church of the Hospital of St Leonard, in honour of the Blessed Virgin Mary and for the souls of the aforesaid William and Isabel his wife and Ivo, father of the said William, and the souls of their ancestors, and of all the faithful deceased for ever.[1]

Owing to its charitable work, this hospital was allowed to continue its legitimate function of poor relief under the auspices of the master, Christopher Massingberd, after the Dissolution. In 1642 a new building was provided by the Dowager Duchess of Exeter to house a master, a chaplain and two poor men. This 'Spittal House' was demolished in 1888 and replaced by four separate houses designed for the residence of two deserving married couples and four single men. These almshouses can still be seen today, inhabited and well cared for.

Recorded evidence for this is a mention of the 'infirmis de Stoke' in the text of the foundation charter. Two hundred years later, in 1315, further mention is made of land gifts at Stoke and Elston by Henry de St Lis, William de Venur and Henry de Sibthorpe. The foundation, dedicated to St Leonard and St Anne, was 'to further the worship of God, and sustain the poor'. Christopher Blackamore has recently put forward convincing evidence that the chapel at Elston was, in fact, the infirmary hall of this hospital.

Harworth

Modern Bawtry lies just across the county boundary in Yorkshire, but the medieval hospital of Bawtry was sited

Elston chapel, part of the ancient hospital site

Rather confusingly a second hospital dedicated to St Leonard was established south of Newark at East Stoke, but the exact site or date has never been verified. Possibly it was an ancient foundation endowed by Ralph Deyncourt in the early 1100s when he established Thurgarton Priory.

south of the town at Harworth, just in Nottinghamshire. This hospital was an early foundation first mentioned in 1200, the dedication being to St Mary Magdalen, and was 'for the sustenance of certain poor persons'. The patronage, at first under Rouen Abbey, was passed to the Archbishops of York until 1390, when the endowment was extended by a charitable benefactor, Robert Morton. At the Dissolution the warden was Richard Pygott, an associate of Henry VIII, an association which helped save the hospital from confiscation. Today the rebuilt parish church of Harworth occupies the site.

Blyth

Whilst it is obvious that many diseases were rife and untreatable in the Middle Ages, leprosy was the dominant cause of disfigurement and suffering. Intensified perhaps by the crusaders' impact of their returning from the East, its spread was explosive. In every case progression of the disease led to gross disfigurement and a slow death. The contagious nature of the illness was soon recognised and segregation of the sufferers enforced. As has already been mentioned, the leper communities were usually outside the town boundary, often near a gate. Not all were endowed, many had no income and were forced to rely on local charity and begging for alms.

Blyth is now a sleepy village, but in the days of the priory it was a bustling community on the Great North Road with two lazar houses. St Edmund's, located to the north, was unendowed. Henry III, while staying there in 1228, hoped that 'his faithful subjects would admit the infirm kindly and hasten to extend charity, so that in addition to eternal reward they might receive the King's gratitude'. A much larger lazar house was established to the south of Blyth in the manor of Hodsock, an early foundation endowed by William de Cressy. The dedication was to St John the Evangelist and the hospital designated for the relief of leprous persons. William appointed a rector and three chaplains. By the middle of the fifteenth century it had passed to the Clifton family, and a plea for contributions recorded for 'the erection and new construction of a certain house in Blyth, for receiving and lodging poor strangers and pregnant women'. On this site, to the south of the long village green, now stands The Spital House Nursing Home, a modern retreat for the old and infirm!

The Bradebusk Hospital, located between Gonalston and Thurgarton on the main Nottingham to Southwell road, exemplified a wayside house. It was dedicated to St Mary

Magdalen by William de Heriz at the end of the twelfth century, and endowed by him for a non-specific number of 'the poor and infirm'. His gifts included a mill and lands at Lowdham, donated for 'the love of God and the souls of his father and mother and of all his ancestors'. A writer at the end of the seventeenth century says of Gonalston: 'Here is a spital or chapel, an ill looking place ... without glass in its windows'.[2] Today even the ruins have disappeared, but Spital Farm House on the site has been reappointed for modern luxury living.

Also dedicated to St Mary Magdalen was a scantily documented hospital at Southwell. A final report on this establishment came from the Commissioners of Henry VIII in 1545. 'The chapel called Mary Magdalen in Easthorpe Fields in the parish of Southwell, by whom or by what intent and purpose it was founded, no man answereth.'[3] The meadow on which it once stood is now in the grounds of Greet House, a formidable edifice, at present lying empty but previously a workhouse.

All this for the love and glorification of God, and to secure for the founder a safe passage to everlasting life.

References

1. C. Brown, *A History of Newark* vol.II (1907), 212

2. R. Thoroton, *The Antiquities of Nottinghamshire* vol.III (2nd ed. by J. Throsby, reprinted Wakefield 1972), 3

3. *Victoria County History of Nottinghamshire*, vol.II, 176

Access
OS SK763 483. Elston chapel, now owned by the Churches Conservation Trust, is marked on most adequate maps of the village and is situated half a mile north-east of the parish church at the end of a lane. It is kept locked, but the key is currently available locally.

The Friaries of Nottingham

Mike Worrall

The two Nottingham Friaries of the Franciscan and the Carmelite Orders present an interesting comparison. Their different characters are seen in their early development, both by the positioning of their sites and in the funding of their land and buildings. There is little evidence of the friaries in the middle period of their existence except where there were transgressions, usually on the part of the leader of the community, and there are but few glimpses of life within them. In Nottingham both orders came to an end on the same day in 1539, by which time there was evidence that the friars had little enthusiasm to continue.

The Friars Minor, or Grey Friars, were first on the scene. Having crossed the Channel in 1220, they went to Oxford after a short stay at Canterbury. It was Franciscan policy to go out in small groups in order to cover the country widely. Within six months three houses had been set up: by 1230 there were twelve, of which Nottingham was one. Typically the friars settled in Broadmarsh, which was low, swampy and undrained - a place where the most deprived population was to be found. It was just outside the town, next to the river Leen. Over the next 80 years there followed a period of building which was assisted largely by the support of Henry III. There being no patron to fund an initial endowment, the king's help must have been vital. Between 1230 and 1302 there were no fewer than ten grants of timber and stone. That year also saw the construction of the 'Frerewatergang', the friars' underground conduit, from the Athilwell near the castle to the friary. In the next year licence for the dedication of the church was given by Archbishop Corbridge, the final dedication of the altar being performed in 1310.

The development of the Carmelite, or White Friars, was quite different. Having been formed on Mount Carmel in the twelfth century, they were 'discovered' in 1238 by Sir Richard Grey and John Vesey who climbed the mountain to visit them while on crusade. Subsequently they were introduced into England in 1240 and appear to have been greatly supported by the Grey family who set up several foundations. One of Richard's descendants, Reginald, Lord Grey of Wilton, founded the Nottingham friary in 1276 together with Sir John Shirley. The site was bounded by Friar Lane and St James Lane within which lay the chapel of St James, once the place where the court of the Honour of Peveril was held, but then belonging to the priory of Lenton. The monks, however, did not hold services there save upon the patron's feast day. The White Friars were not to obtain the chapel until 1316 when the Patent Rolls record:

> Grant to the Carmelite friars of Nottingham of a plot of land with the chapel of St James standing on it in the town of Nottingham, which the king held of the gift of the prior and convent of Lenton, and also of a little lane leading to the said chapel, adjacent to their dwelling-place.[1]

Three years later the Carmelites are recorded as having obtained the 22 properties which lay on Friar Row (the present Beastmarket Hill), Friar Lane (sometime known also as Moot Hall Gate) and St James' Lane (now Street). When these properties had been transferred to them, their occupation and ownership of the 'White Friars' was completed. An unfortunate effect of their owning much of the small parish of St Nicholas was that that church found it had little income to pay its dues, and in 1340 its taxes were reduced specifically for this reason.

There is a little evidence for the religious life of the friars. Thomas of Eccleston noted that, among the achievements of William de Nottingham as prior provincial of the Minors (1250-1254), he 'welcomed a close friendship between our brethren and the Order of Mount Carmel, which had been introduced into England by Lord Richard de Grey when he returned from Syria'[2] In 1291 the Grey Friars were given a mandate to preach the last crusade in Nottingham, Newark and Bingham. There was also a second William of Nottingham, who, while he did not acquire such fame as his earlier namesake, did become the English provincial in the next century. He was buried at Leicester in about 1336.

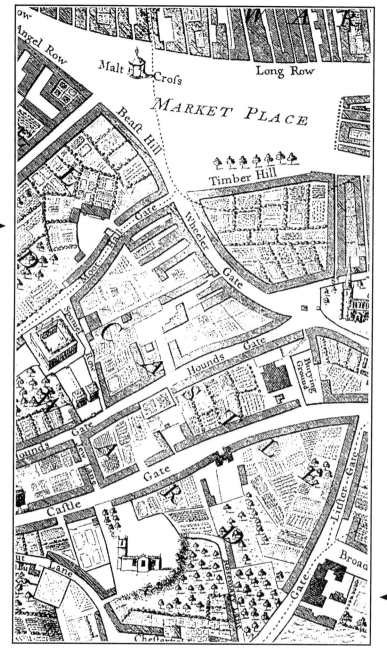

The Carmelite Friary →

← The Franciscan Friary

A section of Badder and Peat's map of Nottingham, 1744, showing the site of
the Carmelite and Franciscan friaries

In 1393 John Leveret, who had killed his wife, fled to the Grey Friars where he was given sanctuary. Both foundations appear to have been held in similar esteem, for when money or goods were left to the friars in wills, it was usually left equally to both.

The common seal of the Nottingham Franciscans showing the town walls and waters of the river Trent

Life cannot have been pleasant in the lower part of Nottingham for the Grey Friars. In 1395 there are several cases brought to the courts about the foul conditions:

> They say that William de Stapleton blocks up with ordure the common street towards the Flexschamulles in the Weekday market on a street which is called Calverton Lane, to the serious detriment of the whole community of the aforesaid town, and to the great obstruction to the water of Leen near Frewatergonge ... to the serious damage of the town aforesaid.[3]

The Carmelites, too, had considerable trouble, though of a different kind. In 1494 the prior was involved in litigation with Thomas Newton, a draper, concerning trespass and fraud. However, in the same year the boot was on the other foot when the prior was sued by his mason, William Stark, for underpayment following repairs to the east window of the chapel. In 1513 the new prior, Thomas Smithson, was similarly sued.

The Grey Friars appear in a more dramatic light on several occasions. In 1402 their warden was arrested for treason at Leicester and charged with sedition against Henry IV. Two years later a friar's head (whose is not clear, for several were involved in the sedition) was ordered to be taken from the town walls. In 1500 Warden William Bell was charged with incontinence as a pimp and in 1521 the warden was accused of 'bawdry with Agnes Waydal'.

The Dissolution came to both friaries on the same day, 5 February 1539. The Grey Friars were surrendered first by the warden, Thomas Barford, and seven brothers. Later that same day Prior Roger Cappe and six others gave up the house of the White Friars. It had been noted just before New Year 1539 that the matter could be accomplished without difficulty, since in a letter it was said 'I am desired to move my Lord for commissions to take the surrender of the friars in ... Nottingham ... for they would fain be gone and the longer they do tarry the more waste they do make'.[4] There seem to be no records of pensions being awarded to the friars. Only Thomas Skevington, who was at one time the warden of the Grey Friars, has been noted, for when he died in the year after the Dissolution he left plate to St Peter's church in whose yard he was buried. The bells of both the friaries are the only items to have been recorded as sold, that from the Grey Friars to Humphrey Quenby, the other of the White Friars to a pewterer.

The Grey Friars' land lay unallotted for nine years until 1548, when it was granted to Sir Thomas Heneage and the heirs of Lord Willoughby. The White Friars' went more quickly to John Sturley (or Strelley, and possibly a descendant of the Shirley who founded them) in 1541. It then went into the possession of the Earls of Rutland, and was associated particularly with Dorothy Vernon of Haddon Hall after her marriage into that family.

Some idea of the buildings and boundaries of the orders can be gained from old maps even though the first, that of John Speed in 1610, is some 70 years after the Dissolution. Speed clearly indicates the Friars' land, though his depiction of houses is less convincing. Thoroton in 1677 neatly shows the buildings of each. The Grey Friars were on the corner of Greyfriar Gate and Broad Marsh, although it has been claimed that the friary had only the western half of the area

T.C. Hine's depiction of Dorothy Vernon's House on the site of the Carmelite Friary in 1892

shown by Speed. By the time of Badder and Peat's map of 1744 there are differently shaped buildings shown on the Greyfriars corner where their house had been and these are annotated as being a lead works. From 1709 the grounds were used for the Abel Collins Almshouses, which later lay to the west of Carrington Street (this had been cut through the site diagonally) and on the north side of Collin Street, i.e., under the western end of today's Broadmarsh Centre.

Archaeological work on the White Friars site, particularly the house off Friar Lane known as Dorothy Vernon's house, in the 1890s, produced evidence of an ancient building which was replaced or partly rebuilt in the seventeenth century. In 1844 bones were found near the corner of St James Street and Beastmarket Hill, which appeared to indicate the site of the friars' burial ground. The house remained until 1927 when it was demolished, but until then

there was an entrance from Friar Lane at exactly the angle of the 'little lane leading to St James's chapel' mentioned in the documents of Edward II which granted the use and ownership of that chapel to the Carmelites. Even now the buildings at the back of the present Barclay's Bank lie at that angle on the site of Dorothy Vernon's house.

References

1. *Calendar of Patent Rolls,* 1313-17, 382

2. J. Burton, *Monastic and Religious Orders in Britain, 1000-1300* (Cambridge, 1994), 114

3. *Records of the Borough of Nottingham* vol.I, 283

4. *Letters and Papers of Henry VIII* vol.14, part I, 229

Newark Friary

Rosemary Robb

The common seal of the Newark Observants showing
St Michael slaying a dragon

The Observants were a late medieval offshoot of the Franciscans, or Grey Friars, whose beliefs in simplicity and poverty they followed to the letter. They represented the upsurge of Catholic piety evident on the eve of the Reformation and their subsequent actions, like those of the Carthusians, showed them to be strong upholders of the papal cause. The Franciscans may have been established in Newark as early as 1291; for in that year they were ordered in Newark, Nottingham and Bingham to supply preachers for the crusade. But beyond that nothing is known.

The Observants were certainly interested in Newark by 1499; for it was one of six towns in which Henry VII ordered a new friary to be built. The Patent Rolls of 1507 refer to laying the 'foundations of a house of the Observant Friars on the site of the ruined chapel of St Saviour with adjacent lands in Newark'. The friary was completed following a bequest of £200 by the king in 1509. Thirty years later, the priory grounds were quoted as measuring 3.2 acres (as they still do), containing a church, garden, two orchards and a cemetery.

The friars must soon have become a familiar sight, dressed in grey habits of coarse cloth with long sleeves, black pointed hoods, and a knotted cord for a girdle. In the under tunics of their habits were large pockets for holding the proceeds of their begging. Unlike monks, they went out to teach and preach among the local people. In all probability they also tended the sick with herbs and potions. They seem to have gained much love and respect from lay people; Thomas Magnus, founder of the Grammar School in Appletongate in 1529, decreed that in choosing deputy masters for the school (to cover in case of illness), the Warden of the Observant Friars was to be consulted. But they also aroused the jealousy and resentment of the secular clergy and other religious orders, especially after papal permission was granted to them to conduct burials, which formed an important source of income for the parish clergy.

The Observants, being dependent on charity, were successful in attracting bequests. Robert Browne left 'Frere Gabriell, father of the house of the Freres Observants of Newark 4d a week and a featherbed'. Richard Bassett of Fledborough left them a legacy to 'pray for my soul and all Christian souls'. From Elizabeth Jenyn of Newark came 15s 'to the building of the Freres'. A bushel of wheat was bequeathed by Robert Hall, and a former registrar from York left 30s. Among the items mentioned in Robert Staunton's will was £100 for his burial, 'at the Friars Observants at Newark-upon-Trent'. He also mentioned a bequest which would enable them to enlarge their church.

In the 1530s the Observants denounced Henry VIII's divorce from Catherine of Aragon so fiercely that they were suppressed, and several friars from the Newark house were to suffer. Their former warden, Gabriel Peacock, who had been transferred to the Southampton Friary, was soon in trouble. The mayor had him arrested after he referred in his sermon in Winchester Cathedral to 'these damned heresies', making clear his objection to the royal claim of supremacy. He was imprisoned at Lincoln. John Barton, a

A wooden image of St Francis in Balderton church, near Newark, believed to have come from the friary

had also befriended the Newark Observants. After being kept in Newgate prison he was detained in the Tower of London and burned at the stake at Smithfield in 1538. Today he is honoured as a Blessed Franciscan martyr.

The royal commissioners received word that the friars Hugh Payn and Thomas Hayfield of Newark had secretly visited Catherine of Aragon when she was in custody at Buckden in Huntingdonshire. They were also accused of mocking the Princess Elizabeth's baptism, declaring that 'the water was not hot enough for her'. Dr Hilsey was sent to Newark to arrest them but found that they had escaped. He tracked them down to Bristol, but by then they had moved on to Devon. Arriving in Devon he found they had fled to Cornwall. Doubling back to Wales, they were eventually captured as their ship was about to sail from Cardiff in July 1534. Payn was imprisoned in London but his companion's fate is unknown. Four years later Bonaventure Roo, who had served at Newark, was betrayed by Richard Lucas, a Newark citizen. Lucas revealed Roo's whereabouts for a bribe of 40s.

For a time after the suppression of the Observants in 1534 Henry VIII installed Austin friars as caretakers of the Newark friary. Then it was given to Richard Andrews and Nicholas Temple and their heirs, and in 1542 passed on to Sir John Markham, a strong supporter of the king. The Markham and Meryng families had been closely associated with the foundation of the friary, and when it was dissolved Sir John Markham's younger brother and Sir William Meryng's younger son were among the community.

Later Sir Francis Leek, a relation of the Markhams, inherited the property. The sale of its gardens, orchards, cemetery, hopyard and pasture fetched only 20s. In the seventeenth century Sir Francis ordered the old house to be pulled down and erected a new building incorporating some of the original stone. This building, with later additions, still stands and is converted into a series of exclusive private flats.

rich merchant from Holme near Newark and a benefactor of Newark Friary, which he later joined, was placed in the custody of the Archbishop of Canterbury. John Ryket, a warden of Newark Friary in 1532, took refuge in Scotland. John Forest, a preacher and advisor to Catherine of Aragon,

---

Access

OS 800539. The site is on Appletongate, near the town centre. Part of the Friary grounds are now a public park.

'The Friary' apartments at Newark

Epilogue

David Marcombe

anctity and Scandal is the work of the Archdeaconry Research Unit, a group of volunteer researchers based at the University of Nottingham's Centre for Local History, School of Continuing Education, since 1980. By any definition we are an odd mix of individuals; even odder looked at in the context of most people's preconceptions of university 'boffins'. True, we have in the group a retired university lecturer and, indeed, a history graduate from Oxford; but there is also a former tax inspector, two retired GPs, and a teacher, librarian and secretary who are still at work, balancing the demands of research against family, career and other commitments. What many members of the research team have in common is successful completion of one of the University's qualifications in local history. Two contributors to this volume are graduates of the MA course; and thirteen have successfully completed the Advanced Certificate. Some, on the other hand, have done neither and their contribution to the finished product is no less valuable because of that. Most important of all, we are friends.

How has such a diverse group been moulded into a coherent research team? With remarkable ease it must be said. The Archdeaconry Research Unit is a democratic group with a mind of its own and the task of its leader has been to ride the surf rather than to channel the efforts of the group along rigidly predetermined paths. In the end things get done quietly and efficiently. Negotiation and compromise have been the hallmarks of our success and over the eighteen years of its existence ARU (as it has become known) has notched up achievements to be proud of. First, the extraction of a huge amount of data from the court books of the Archdeacons of Nottingham. Second, a book on Retford, *English Small Town Life,* put together by the leader but resting heavily on research by the team. And

now, *Sanctity and Scandal,* an analysis of the medieval religious houses of Nottinghamshire.

As the group assembled to put the finishing touches to this most recent effort, someone reminded us that it had taken all of eight years to complete. In terms of a narrow research focus the timescale could, no doubt, have been much shorter, but in reality ARU does more than just research. It organises field visits, lectures, social events and in recent years it has been pro-active in initiating a Research Forum in an attempt to draw together historians across the East Midlands working on local projects, not necessarily in a university context. And then there are the inevitable hiccoughs resulting from busy people leading busy lives. A researcher moves away to Somerset; a file of papers is left on a bus; changed family circumstances take their toll. Another reason for the extended timescale was that the group was involved creatively with the publication process almost up to the last step, debating decisions over content, layout, illustrations, referencing and a host of other practicalities. The truth is, time passes quickly when you are enjoying yourself and learning is nothing if it is not fun.

If the project was a mind-broadening exercise in the best sense of the word, unexpected talents were developed *en route.* Specialists soon emerged in the fields of art history and monastic economy. It transpired that the husbands of two members of the group were talented artists who were prepared to help us with line drawings. One member obtained a flight in an aeroplane to take pictures of Shelford Priory; another honed an interest in dowsing and through patient and skilful work reconstructed the first plans of Welbeck Abbey and Felley Priory to be seen since the sixteenth century. Because of these varied enthusiasms and the different amounts of time people have been able to put into them, the essays are uneven, and deliberately so, for we set out to reflect the interests and aptitudes of individuals within a generally agreed set of guidelines. The work on Premonstratensian Visitations is perhaps somewhat tangental to the main thrust of the book, but we all felt that it shed sufficient light on themes of general interest to be allowed to stand virtually unaltered.

Within this rich diversity our agreed aim has been to write a history and guide to the Nottinghamshire monasteries which is comprehensible to the average non-academic reader and which reflects the enthusiasm we all felt for the subject of our choice. You must judge whether or not we have been successful in this. Certainly Nottinghamshire has been neglected too long as a county with a monastic heritage to be proud of. Some of the monks' churches are still in use for their intended purpose today. It was wonderful, for example, to see Walter Hilton being commemorated with lectures and medieval-style liturgy at Thurgarton in 1996. Others are being adapted for the tourist market as Nottinghamshire County Council is successfully demonstrating at Rufford. Sadly, some are in a shameful state of decay. Beauvale's walls can be allowed to crumble no longer. Something must be done soon or they will fall down. The case of Newark Friary, where the new 'gentry' of the town pay London-style prices for appartments carved out of the domain of the impoverished Observants, is an issue for the sociologist rather than the historian. But interesting, nevertheless.

The fact that *Sanctity and Scandal* has been written does not mean that the last word has been said about the Nottinghamshire monasteries, by any means. As stated above, this is a lay person's history. With more time and more space the story of most of these monasteries could be filled out to a much greater extent. Trevor Foulds's work on Thurgarton Priory proves the point, if any proof is required. If potential researchers are not attracted by the prospect of an in-depth study of a particular house, our 'overview' approach might usefully be applied to adjacent counties, such as Leicestershire and Derbyshire, which have a comparable monastic heritage. Anyone wishing to tackle Lincolnshire would need a much bigger book, but that does not mean that the initiative would not be an extremely productive one. It is hoped, therefore, that ARU has shown the way ... that we have put the Nottinghamshire monasteries 'on the map' and lit a candle so that others might follow the path. We look forward to our next project with relish ... whatever, wherever, it might be!

Angelic musician from the choir stalls at Thurgarton

Glossary

Joy Bristow

abbey	A monastery governed by an abbot or abbess
abbot	The elected head of a convent
advowson	Right of presentation to an ecclesiastical benefice
alien house	Owing obedience to a mother house in a foreign country
alienate (property)	The transfer by sale or inheritance, of a property, from one owner to another
almoner	Religious person who dispenses alms, food and drink to the poor
ambry	Niche in a church for holding books and sacred utensils
apostasy	Abandonment or breaking of religious vows
appurtenance	Land or buildings annexed to another
apse/apsidal	Semicircular or polygonal east end of a chancel or side chapel
arcade	Series of arches carried on columns or piers; a passage arched over; a covered walk
assart	Enclosure or clearing of forest or waste land
assize of bread and ale	Statutory regulation for fixing the price of bread and ale
attaint/attainder	Forfeiture of lands and possessions for treason so that heirs are unable to inherit
Augmentations, Court of	Institution set up by Thomas Cromwell to administer the revenues of dissolved religious houses and also to pay pensions to the displaced monks
bestiary	A book containing animal stories and pictures
bovate	The area of land that an ox could plough in a year; generally taken to be about twenty acres in the East Midlands

camera	An estate belonging to a commandery (qv)
canons regular	Communities of priests following a monastic rule
cantor	Director of music
cartulary	Collection of charters relating to a particular estate
carucate	Measure of land, as much as could be ploughed by one plough and eight oxen in a year, the amount varying with the condition of soil. Generally believed to be about 120 acres
cellarer	Monk in charge of the *cellarium*, a store house for food and drink; also in charge of business affairs of the house
censer	Or thurible, metal vessels used for the burning of incense
chalice	Vessel used for communion
chantry	Chapel where masses were performed for the souls of the dead in Purgatory
chapter	Daily assembly of a religious community for the reading of a chapter from the *Rule* of the Order. The body of the religious members of a community
chapter house	Room, often situated adjacent to the church on the east side of the cloister, where the monks met daily to conduct monastic business
circator	Monk responsible for inspection 'rounds' day and night
clerestory	Range of high windows along the central walls of a church above the aisle roof
cloister	A square covered walkway along the inner walls of a monastery usually built round a garden/courtyard
commandery	A house of the Knights of St John of Jerusalem directed by an officer known as a 'commander'
commissary-general	A representative of the bishop, a chief or head commissary
convent	Community of religious persons, male or female
conventual church/buildings	Of, or belonging to, a religious house or convent
corrodian	One who enjoys a corrody (qv)

corrody	Contract between a lay person and a monastic community for maintenance of the corrodian (qv)
Court of Augmentations	Institution set up by Thomas Cromwell to administer the revenues of dissolved religious houses and also to pay pensions to the displaced monks
custos grangie	Administrator of the abbey granges or farms
demesne	That part of a monastic estate farmed directly by the monks and not leased or let out
denizen	A person who lives in a country, but is not native born
dog-tooth decoration	A series of ornamental pyramid-like projections often over a door
doom painting	A wall painting which provided a teaching aid for parishioners who were unable to read. It depicted the Day of Judgement, with the good souls going to Heaven, and the sinners to Hell
dorter	The dormitory of the monks
dowsing	Searching for subterranean water or building remains by means of a divining rod, often of metal, sometimes a forked stick of some fruit- bearing wood, generally hazel
encaustic tiles	Tiles of a patterned, two-tone colour, produced by an imprint in clay, filled with slip (liquid clay) before firing
enfeoffed	Possessed of land or other property under a superior lord
farm	Block letting for fixed payment for a number of years, applied not only to land but to tithes, rents, fines, etc., let to a 'farmer'
fee	The area of jurisdiction subject to feudal obligations
feudal	Holding of land by feudal tenure
fother (of lead)	A measure of weight, varied from 22.5 cwt in Derbyshire to 19.5 cwt in London. Also fodder and fudder
frater	The eating place in a monastery
garderobe	Latrine or privy, often built into the thickness of an exterior wall, draining into a pit, river or moat
garth	An open central area overlooked by the cloisters

Gregorian chant	A form of monastic plainsong modified by Pope Gregory the Great
groin-vaulted	An angular curve formed by the intersection of two vaults
hermit	A religious person living in seclusion, also called an anchorite/anchoress
hermitage	Home of a hermit (qv)
honour	A large estate consisting of several manors
incontinence	Adultery or fornication
lady chapel	A chapel dedicated to the Virgin Mary
lancet	A narrow window with a pointed head in the Early English style
lay brother	Monastic servant subject to the same discipline as the choir monks, but usually unlettered, responsible for the day-to-day servicing of the community
magister grangie	See 'custos grangie'
mark	Medieval unit of accounting. In England, after the Conquest (1066), the ratio of 20 sterling pennies to an ounce was the basis of computation; hence the value of a mark became fixed at 160 pennies = 13s 4d. Thus half a mark = 6s 8d
maundy money	Dole of money given out on Maundy Thursday, the day before Good Friday
messuage	Dwelling house and its appurtenances, i.e. outbuildings, garden and in some instances land
misericord	Recreational area of a monastery, sometimes known as the 'warming house' (qv). Also the seat of a choir stall, often decorated on the underside
mullion	A dividing upright between the lights of windows, panels, etc.
nook shaft	A shaft placed in the internal angle of a wall
obedientiary	The monk in charge of the administrative sections of the community, such as the cellarer, the infirmarian or the sacrist
obit	An annual commemoration, usually a Mass, commending to God a deceased person, especially a founder or benefactor
officinarius in pistrino	Monk in charge of the mill and/or bakery

pannage	The right or privilege of feeding pigs or other animals in a wood
patron	A person who supports the monastery by the giving of land and money
pentice/pentise	A small sacred building dependent upon a larger church. A passage or corridor along the side of a building, with a single pitch roof
piscina	A carved basin with a drain, set into church wall, in which sacred vessels were washed
pontage	A toll paid for the use, maintenance or repair of a bridge
precentor	See 'cantor'
preceptory	A house of the Knights Templars directed by an officer known as a 'preceptor'. An alternative term for commandery, e.g. in the *Valor Ecclesiasticus*
presbytery	The eastern arm of the church which contains the enclosure of the high altar to the east of the monks' choir stalls
prior	Head of priory; in an abbey second in command responsible for maintenance of order
priory	Monastery or convent governed by a prior or prioress. In England the normal term for a religious house
proctor	The person who collects alms on behalf of those who are unable to beg for themselves, especially for the occupants of an almshouse
provincial (office)	The ecclesiastical head of a province, the chief of a religious order in a district or province
provisor exteriorum	Steward of the outside
pulpitum	A stone or wood screen in a church separating the choir from the nave
purgation/purge	The procedure for the moral or spiritual cleansing of a person especially after sexual transgression
quatrefoil	Having four leaves or four parts
quit-claim	Release and disclaimer of all rights, interest and potential legal actions from a grantor to a grantee
redditio	Latin for payment, giving up, surrendering
refectory	The room used for communal meals

reredorter	A privy or latrine situated at the back of a dormitory, flushed by running water
reredos	An ornamental or decorated screen behind an altar
responsion	A fixed proportion of the revenue paid by commanders of military orders to the convent (headquarters) of the order. It was usually assessed at a third of the net income but was liable to be increased in emergencies
rood-screen	The screen that separated the nave from the chancel. Often set directly to the east of the nave altar
sacrist	The monastic official responsible for the sacred vessels, the altars and the fabric of the church
scapula	Part of the monk's dress, it consisted of a broad band of cloth open at the sides and hanging down front and back. It was worn over their habit, and usually worn when engaged in manual labour
scriptorium	The room or other place in a religious house set apart for writing and the copying of manuscripts
sedilia	A recessed row of seats for use by the clergy, often crowned with canopies or pinnacles, usually on the south side of the choir near to the altar
ship of silver	A vessel in the shape of a boat, containing the incense. When required a little of the incense was taken out with a spoon made for the purpose, and incense was thrown on the burning charcoal in the censer (qv)
simony	The sale of ecclesiastical preferment, or particular religious objects, a practice regarded as sinful
slype	The covered way or passage usually leading from the cloister to the cemetery
spiritualities or spiritual income	Revenue arising from ecclesiastical sources, such as tithes, church court fees and religious pensions (see also temporalities)
succentor	Assistant to cantor/precentor (qv)
Tau cross	A Greek letter shaped like a 'T' sometimes used as a substitute for a cross
Taxatio	The valuation of all ecclesiastical property for taxation purposes by the order of Pope Nicholas IV in 1291
Temple	The name initially given to the more important houses of the Templars

temporalities	Income arising from secular sources such as buildings, lands, gifts of money (see also spiritualities)
tithe	The tenth part of all produce, stock and labour, and of business/trade profits, to be paid to the parish church as a religious due. Monasteries were generally exempted from this payment but were collectors of it
tonsure	A monastic haircut producing a bald patch in the centre of the skull, sometimes said to resemble Christ's crown of thorns
transept	One arm of the crossing in a cruciform church
triforium	Blank arcading, gallery or wall passage between the top of the main arcade and the clerestory above
undercroft	An underground crypt below a church, or any chamber beneath a major building
underwood	Small trees or shrubs, coppice-wood or brush wood growing beneath higher trees
Valor Ecclesiasticus	A survey of church property in England and Wales undertaken following a parliamentary decree in 1535.
vellum	Very fine parchment prepared from the skins of calves, and used especially for writing, painting or binding. Also any superior quality of parchment
vill	A small administrative area, the Norman-French equivalent of the Old English township
villein	Unfree but land-holding peasant of early feudal times
visitation	A visit by an ecclesiastical person to examine the state of a religious institution
visitor	An ecclesiastic or lay commissioner appointed to inspect religious establishments, either at regular intervals or on special occasions, usually the bishop or a senior prior of the order
wapentake	A subdivision of certain 'Danelaw' East Midland shires, corresponding to the 'Hundred' in other parts of the country
warming house	Or *calefactorium,* the room containing a large fireplace, where the monks were able to warm themselves during the winter months
warren (free)	The right of keeping or hunting beasts and fowls of warren. These included hares, rabbits, roes, partridge, pheasant and woodcock

Bibliography

PRIMARY SOURCES

Published PRO Calendars, including the *Charter Rolls, Close Rolls, Fine Rolls, Patent Rolls, Inquisitions Post Mortem, Quo Warranto, Letters and Papers Foreign and Domestic of Henry VIII,* and the *Calendars of Papal Registers and Letters*

Pipe Rolls (published by the Pipe Rolls Society)

Publications of the Surtees Society *Registers of the Archbishops of York: Corbridge,* I,138, (1925), II, 141, (1928); *Giffard,* 109, (1904); *Greenfield,* I, 145, (1931), II, 149, (1934), III, 152, (1936), IV, 153, (1937), V, 154, (1938); *Gray,* 56, 1870; *Romeyn,* I, 123, (1913), II, 128, (1916); *Wichwane,* 114, (1907)

S. Aynscough and J. Caley (ed.), *Taxatio Ecclesiastica Angliae (The Taxatio of Pope Nicholas IV), 1291,* (London 1802)

J. Caley, (ed.), *Valor Ecclesiasticus of Henry VIII* 5, (1825)

All the above official royal and ecclesiastical papers have been published and are available in major libraries

J.P.H. Clark and R. Dorward (eds), *Walter Hilton: The Scale of Perfection* (Paulist Press, 1991)

R. Dorward (trans.), *Walter Hilton: 8 Chapters on Perfection and Angels' Song* (1983)

F.A. Gasquet (ed.), *Collectanea Anglo-Premonstratensia,* 1, 2, 3 (Camden Society, 3rd series, 1904-6)

L.B. Larking (ed.), *Knights Hospitallers in England, being the Report of Prior Philip de Thame to the Grand Master Elyan de Villanova for AD 1338* (Camden Society, 1857)

W.H. Stephenson (ed.), *Records of the Borough of Nottingham* 1-3 (Bernard Quaritch, London, 1882)

F.B. Stitt (ed.), 'Lenton Priory Estate Accounts, 1296-1298', *Thoroton Society Record Series,* 19, 1959

Nottinghamshire Cartularies

T. Foulds (ed.), *Thurgarton Cartulary* (Paul Watkins, Stamford, 1996)

D. Gray (ed.), 'Newstead Priory Cartulary 1344 and other archives', trans. V W Walker, *Thoroton Society Record Series,* 8, 1940

C.J. Holdsworth (ed.), 'Rufford Charters, 1 - 3', *Thoroton Society Record Series,* 24, 1972; 30, 1974; 32, 1980

R.T. Timson (ed.), 'The Cartulary of Blyth Priory', *Thoroton Society Record Series,* 27, 1973

SECONDARY SOURCES

TTS = Transactions of the Thoroton Society

Individual Houses

Lenton

F.A. Barnes, 'Lenton Priory after the Dissolution: its buildings and fairgrounds', *TTS* 91, 1987-8

F.A. Barnes, *Priory Demesne to University Campus* (Nottingham 1993)

B.W. Beilby, 'Excavations at the Cluniac Priory of the Holy Trinity Lenton 1962-1964', *TTS* 70, 1966

R.H. Elliott and A.E. Burbank, 'Lenton Priory Excavations 1943-1951', *TTS* 56, 1952

J.T. Godfrey, *The History of the Parish and Priory of Lenton* (London and Derby, 1884)

H. Green, 'The History of Lenton Priory', *TTS* 40, 1936

D. Marcombe, 'The Last Days of Lenton Priory', in D. Wood (ed.), *Life and Thought in the Northern Church, c.1100-c.1700: essays in honour of Claire Cross,* Studies in Church History, 12 (Boydell and Brewer, 1998)

H.H. Swinnerton and H. Boulton, 'Lenton Priory Excavations in 1954', *TTS* 60, 1956

Thurgarton

T. Foulds, *Thurgarton Priory and its Benefactors; with an edition of the cartulary* (PhD thesis, University of Nottingham, 1984)

T. Foulds, 'The History of Thurgarton Priory before 1316', *TTS* 84, 1980

See also the *Introduction to the Thurgarton Cartulary* listed above

Others

A.M.Y. Baylay, 'Annesley Old Church' and 'Felley Priory', *TTS* 16, 1912

C. Blackamore, *'Elston Chapel and St Leonard's Hospital at East Stoke',* (Advanced Certificate in Local History Dissertation, University of Nottingham, 1994)

R.E.G. Cole, 'The priory, or house of nuns, of St Mary of Broadholme, of the order of Premontre', Lincoln Archaeological Society, in *Associated Societies Reports and Papers,* 28, 1907

C. Cross, 'The Reconstitution of Northern Monastic Communities in the reign of Mary Tudor', *Northern History,* 29, 1993

J.M. Greasley, *The Austin Priory of St Mary of Newstead in Sherwood, Nottinghamshire* (1861)

J.R.H. Moorman, *The Franciscans in England* (Mowbrays, London, 1974)

J. Raine, *The History and Antiquities of the Parish of Blyth* (Westminster, 1860)

P. Stephens, *Grey Sanctuary: the story of the Newark Friary* (Nottinghamshire County Council, 1996)

A. Hamilton Thompson, *The Premonstratensian Abbey at Welbeck* (Faber and Faber, London 1938)

E.M. Thompson, *The Carthusian Order in England* (SPCK, London, 1930)

V.W.Walker (revised M.L. Howell), *The House of Byron* (Quiller Press, London, 1988)

M.H. Towry White, 'Some Account of the Family of White of Tuxford and Wallingwells', *TTS* 11, 1907

General Works

G. Baskerville, *English Monks and the Supression of the Monasteries* (Cape, London, 1937)

J. Bramley, *A short History of the Religious Houses of Nottinghamshire to the time of the Dissolution* (Milward & Sons, 1948)

C. Brown, *A History of Newark-on-Trent,* 2 vols (Newark 1904/7)

A. Cameron, 'Some social Consequences of the Dissolution of the Monasteries in Nottinghamshire', *TTS* 79-80, 1975-6

G. Coppack, *The English Heritage Book of Abbeys and Priories* (B T Batsford, London, 1990)

A. Cossons, 'The Pensioned Priests of Nottinghamshire', *TTS* 44, 1940

C.M.D. Deering, *History of Nottingham* (S R Publications, Wakefield, 1970, reprint of *Nottinghamia vetus et nova* of 1751).

J.C. Dickenson, *Monastic Life in Medieval England* (Black, 1961)

J.C. Dickenson, *The Origins of the Austin Canons and their introduction to England* (SPCK London, 1950)

W. Dugdale, *Monasticon Anglicanum,* 6 vols (London, 1817)

F.A. Gasquet, *Henry VIII and the English Monasteries,* 2 vols (London, 1893)

B. Golding, *Gilbert of Sempringham and the Gilbertine Order c.1130-c.1300,* (Clarendon Press, 1995)

E.J. King, *The Knights of St John in the British Empire: Being the Official History of the Most Venerable Order of the Hospital of St John of Jerusalem,* 3rd ed., (London, 1990)

L. Jacks, *The Great Houses of Nottinghamshire and the County Families* (Nottingham, 1881)

D. Knowles, *The English Mystical Tradition* (Burns and Oates, 1961)

D. Knowles, *The Religious Orders in England,* 3 vols (C.U.P., Cambridge, 1955-62)

D Knowles, *The Monastic Order in England,* 2nd ed. (C.U.P., Cambridge, 1963)

D. Knowles and R.N. Hadcock, *Medieval Religious Houses: England and Wales,* 2nd ed. (Longman, 1971)

C.H. Lawrence, *Medieval Monasticism: Forms of Religious Life in Western Europe in the Middle Ages,* 2nd ed. (Longman, 1989)

A.G. Little (ed.), *Franciscan History and Legend in English Mediaeval Art* (Manchester University Press, 1937)

W. Page (ed.), *Victoria History of the Counties of England: Nottinghamshire,* 2 (Folkestone and London 1910, reprinted 1970); usually known as the *Victoria County History of Nottinghamshire*

N. Pevsner, *The Buildings of England series Nottinghamshire* (Penguin, 1951)

R. Thoroton, *The Antiquities of Nottinghamshire,* 2nd ed. edited and enlarged by J. Throsby (reprinted E.P. Publishing, Wakefield, 1972)

A. Stapleton, *The Churches and Monasteries of Old and New Nottingham* (Nottingham, 1903)

W. Stephenson and A. Stapleton, *Some Account of the Religious Institutions of Old Nottingham* (Nottingham, 1895)

J. Walsh (ed.), *Pre-Reformation English Spirituality* (1965)

R. White, *The Dukery Records* (published privately, 1904)

A.C. Wood, *Nottinghamshire in the Civil War* (Oxford, 1937)

Index

The index does not claim to be comprehensive; founders have been listed, as have those who bought properties after the Dissolution. However, individuals in the various religious houses and the lay people with whom they came in contact, have not been listed.